Caring Enough To Lead

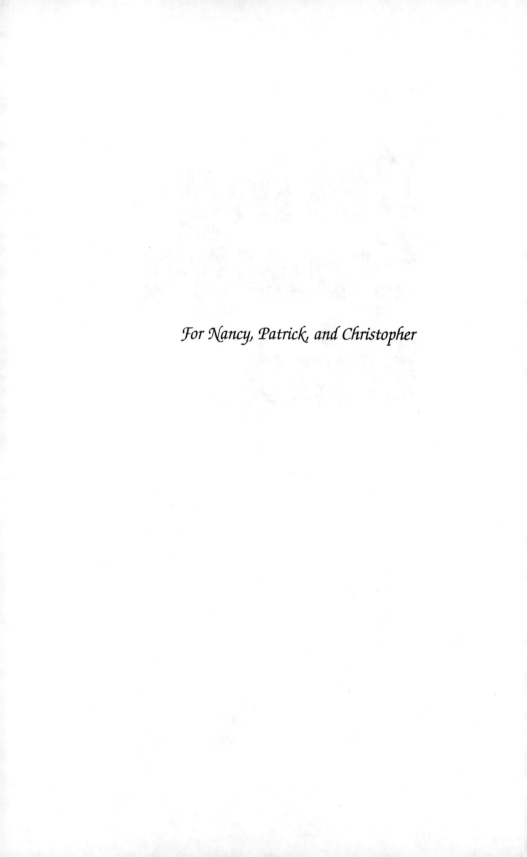

For Nancy, Patrick, and Christopher

Caring Enough To Lead

How Reflective Thought Leads to Moral Leadership
Second Edition

Foreword by Richard W. Riley
Former U.S. Secretary of Education

Leonard O. Pellicer

CORWIN PRESS, INC.
A Sage Publications Company
Thousand Oaks, California

For information:

Corwin Press, Inc.
A Sage Publications Company
2455 Teller Road
Thousand Oaks, California 91320
www.corwinpress.com

Sage Publications Ltd.
6 Bonhill Street
London EC2A 4PU
United Kingdom

Sage Publications India Pvt. Ltd.
B-42, Panchsheel Enclave
Post Box 4109
New Delhi 110 017 India

Printed in the United States of America

Library of Congress Cataloging-in-Publication Data

Pellicer, Leonard O.

Caring enough to lead: How reflective thought leads to moral leadership/ Leonard O. Pellicer.—2nd ed.

    p. cm

Includes bibliographical references and index.

ISBN 0-7619-3878-8 (Cloth)

ISBN 0-7619-3879-6 (Paper)

    1. Educational leadership—United States. 2. School management and organization—United States. 3. School principals—United States. 4. School administrators—United States. I. Title.

LB2805.P375 2003

371.2—dc21

               2003001714

This book is printed on acid-free paper.

03   04   05   06   10 9 8 7 6 5 4 3 2 1

Acquisitions Editor:	Robert D. Clouse
Associate Editor:	Kristen L. Gibson
Editorial Assistant:	Jingle Vea
Production Editor:	Denise Santoyo
Copy Editor:	Carla Freeman
Typesetter:	C&M Digitals (P) Ltd.
Indexer:	Kay Dusheck
Cover Designer:	Tracy E. Miller
Production Artist:	Lisa Miller

Contents

Foreword to the First Edition vii
  Aretha B. Pigford

Foreword to the Second Edition xi
  Governor Richard W. Riley

Preface xiii

About the Author xxiii

1. It's Better to Know Some of the
   Questions Than All the Answers 1

2. Why Am I Going to Visit Bob? 7

3. What Is a Leader? 13

4. What Do I Care About? 27

5. What Do I Believe About People? 37

6. Am I Willing to Share Power? 47

7. Do I Care Enough to Do the Little Things? 57

8. What Does It Mean to Be Responsible? 67

9. Am I Willing to Jump for the Brass Ring? 75

10. Am I Taking Care of My Water Buffalo? 85

11. Why Am I Doing This? 91

12. Who's the King or Queen of the Jungle? 101

13. Honey, Do These Pants Make Me Look Fat? 107

14. What Does It Mean to Be a Teacher? 115

15. Can You Just Call Me Willie, Mrs. Peterson? 121

16. Can I Care Enough to Be My Own Best Friend? 129

17. Why Haven't Our Schools Been
    More Successful? 137

18. How Is a School Transformed? 145

19. Why Am I a Professional Educator? 157

20. Will That Be a Senior Coffee? 167

21. Your Leadership Becomes You! 179

References 187

Index 191

Foreword to
the First Edition

A few years ago, I received an incredible gift: the opportunity to participate in a leadership development program sponsored by the Kellogg Foundation. This three-year experience allowed me to visit cultures throughout the world and explore leadership firsthand. My explorations took me to a quaint Amish community in Pennsylvania; to a dirt-poor sugar cane plantation in Costa Rica; to a cramped township in South Africa; to a condemned public housing project in Houston; and to an opulent presidential palace in Central America. During my journey, I observed the leadership of the rich and powerful as well as the poor and victimized. I met with internationally acclaimed Nobel Peace Prize recipients, with impoverished Chiapa women weavers, with embittered South African students, and with grief-stricken Guatemalan mothers.

My mission was simple: to observe and analyze leadership and attempt to reach some conclusions about this elusive phenomenon. As I began my journey, I did so acknowledging that the study of leadership was nothing new to me. As a former graduate student in educational administration, I was steeped in leadership theory. As a professor of educational administration, I had spent more than ten years teaching leadership classes. As a former principal, assistant dean, and associate superintendent, I had numerous opportunities to practice leadership. But this journey took me down a new path, a path that challenged me to see leadership from a different perspective, a path that shifted my focus from the "behaviors" to the "being" of leadership.

By the end of my journey, I had reached several conclusions, the most definitive of which was simple, but profound: Authentic leaders are people who do what they do because of a genuine desire to make things better for others. The fact that a personal sacrifice might be required does not stop them. Simply stated, they care enough to lead. Caring enough—that is the primary motivation for authentic leadership as well as the essential message of this book. Filled with anecdotes and vignettes, *Caring Enough to Lead* provides a powerful account of Leonard Pellicer's personal journey into leadership. Through a series of intriguing, insightful questions, Leonard challenges us to take an introspective, reflective journey into ourselves, the first step toward becoming an authentic leader. Unlike the typical book on leadership, *Caring* is not about doing; there are no checklists of behaviors. It is about "being."

The author is eminently qualified to write about leadership, not because of his impressive academic credentials, but because of his life experiences and his unique ability to create meaning from them. Whether by choice or circumstance, Leonard's life has been characterized by being out front. Throughout his life, in a great variety of formal and informal leadership roles, he has continued to inspire a host of willing followers. Why are persons so willing to follow him? During our twenty-year association, I have observed the following. First, he regards leadership as a sacred trust given to him by willing followers. He respects and honors that trust. Second, he listens to all the voices and, when necessary, gives voice to those who are silent or marginalized. Third, he is not afraid to push the limits and inspires those who fear leaving the security of their comfort zones to do likewise. Most importantly, he understands fully that leadership is about service—not about power.

Caring Enough to Lead is Leonard's personal gift to us. In it, he lets his guard down and allows us to observe him as he takes inventory of himself, with the hope that we will be challenged to do likewise. It is only by doing so that each of us can begin the journey to authentic leadership.

—Aretha B. Pigford

Foreword to
the Second Edition

As Governor of South Carolina in the 1980s and then as U.S. Secretary of Education in the 1990s, I had the great fortune to be a leader in education. Imagine the overwhelming feeling of making decisions that would impact all children of a state or of our great nation.

What, then, are the characteristics of leadership that could best serve a person facing this heavy responsibility? Well, it isn't a feeling of power and importance. It isn't even experience, though knowledge of the subject is important. And it certainly isn't the self-confidence to give orders to your employees, expecting and demanding that they be carried out. No, it's more than all of that, and that is what my friend Leonard Pellicer understands and shares with us in this second edition of his book, *Caring Enough to Lead*.

I first knew Leonard as an outstanding principal of a high school in my home school district. His reputation as a special kind of school leader had already been established. He was about the work of "being" a school leader. He worked in the area of staff development for teachers and administrators in Florida; he was a Fulbright Scholar, training school leaders in the Philippines; and he continued his education leadership teaching postsecondary educators.

Caring Enough to Lead is based upon Leonard Pellicer's three-plus decades of varied experience as a professional educator. He has not only served, but he has observed and listened and recorded what he has learned.

Yes, he has learned the importance of education as a building block for our democracy and as the key building block for every child's future. He believes in the power of education for human and societal development. And he cares enough to fight for his beliefs.

And here again, he is sharing his conviction about leadership with us in a very personal and practical way: his touching story about his visits with his friend who was struggling with Alzheimer's disease; his observations about the rhythms of the farmer in the Philippines leading and guiding the powerful water buffalo; the difficulty of making tough choices when asked by a woman if "these pants make me look too fat"—that is, truth versus sensitivity to one's feelings. All these stories approach the subject of leadership in a creative and interesting way.

One of the most revealing stories is about transforming a low-performing school. Zenia Elementary School was such a school until it gained a caring principal who had a simple but powerful vision: No child will fail. The principal built a staff and entire school community that shared that vision. He cared enough to lead, and it made a real difference in the lives of all children fortunate enough to attend Zenia Elementary School.

In order to help the reader internalize the meaning he is portraying, the author has included a set of reflective exercises at the end of each chapter. These exercises make readers realize that, indeed, they are the ones to whom the book speaks. And by applying these ideas to one's own involvement in education and one's own life, you can begin "dancing the dance of a leader" who cares enough to lead.

—Governor Richard W. Riley

Preface

Some other faculty than the intellect is necessary for the apprehension of reality.

—Henri Bergson

Purpose of the Book

No one who takes the time to read *Caring Enough to Lead* will mistake it for a textbook. Rather than a rehash of the tenets of leadership according to a host of theoreticians past and present, the book presents a personal perspective on what it means to care enough to lead. Beyond the briefest introduction, this book is not the least bit concerned with leadership theory and the organizational structures, processes, and rational technical skills that flow from it, but rather with an understanding of who we are as leaders and what we can become as we bond with others in meaningful ways to help transform our nation's schools.

The discussion of leaders and leadership is thousands of years old. Men, women, and even children have been leading for as long as human beings have banded together and worked cooperatively, initially in an effort to survive and later to improve the quality of life. Countless studies have tried to determine what causes or allows some people to lead and others to follow. Although much has been learned about leaders and leading, for the most part, leadership remains an intriguing mystery.

Throughout the last century, the literature has demonstrated some interesting twists and turns in the study of leadership and the posing of leadership theories. Beginning with the *great man theory* (as far as I can determine, there was no great woman theory), which postulates that leaders are born and not made, the study of leadership has progressed through a series of distinct phases as thinking about leaders and leadership has become more sophisticated, if not more valid.

The *traits theory*, the successor to the great man theory, suggests that the behaviors of successful leaders can be attributed to a set of unique personality traits such as forcefulness, intelligence, and need for achievement. The development of measurement in the field of psychology coincided with and provided the impetus for the idea of studying leaders by measuring the presence or absence of certain traits, using tools such as checklists, tests, rating scales, and interviews.

The work of Frederick Taylor in the early twentieth century gave rise to a school of thinkers in the field of leadership studies who have been described as *behavioral theorists*. The behavioral theorists include a distinguished list of notables, such as Argyris, Blake, Mouton, Getzels, Guba, Likert, and McGregor. These researchers believed that what leaders do is far more significant than any set of traits they might possess, and consequently they focused their research on the development of leadership styles and leader behavior. The behaviorists recognize that although organizations might be rigid, human beings within those organizations have needs that must be addressed if the organizations are to be productive. From the work of the behavioral theorists came a series of leadership models, assessment tools, and motivational theories that have had enormous influence on the study and practice of leadership right up to the present day.

Situational leadership theory evolved during the 1960s from the work of the behavioral theorists and questions whether or not there is one best way for a leader to lead in all situations. Situational theorists such as Fiedler, Hersey, and Blanchard maintain that effective leadership behavior is dependent on the situation in which the leader operates and must take into account variables such as the nature of the tasks to be performed, the maturity of the group, and operative time constraints. Situational leadership theory emphasizes the need to alter approaches to leadership based on the circumstances present in a particular situation to realize optimal results.

Transformational leadership theory came into its own in the late 1970s and continues to be explored up until the present. Transformational leadership theory seeks to explain the relationships among leaders and others in an organization when they are engaged in such a way that the organization is raised to a higher plane of morality and maturity and is thereby transformed. Transformation can be achieved by a variety of means but generally occurs when individuals in an organization are able to transcend their own self-interests for the sake of the organization and its clients. Transformational leaders help their colleagues identify their common core values and attach these values to designated organizational outcomes that are highly prized by the group. *Visionary, inspirational, charismatic, intellectual,* and *authentic* are common terms that have been used to describe transformational leaders. With the recent emphasis on organizational restructuring in business and industry as well as in schools, transformational leadership has assumed a central place in the literature on leadership. The following are some of the more popular recent titles that illustrate the current fascination with transformational leadership: *Leading With Soul: An Uncommon Journey of Spirit* (Bolman & Deal, 1995); *Stewardship: Choosing Service Over Self-Interest* (Block, 1993); *The Loyalty Effect* (Reichheld, 1996); *Moral Leadership: Getting to the Heart of School Improvement* (Sergiovanni, 1992); *Managing From the Heart* (Bracey, Rosenblum, Sanford, & Trueblood, 1990); *Managing by Values* (Blanchard & O'Connor, 1997); and *Leading*

Without Power: Finding Hope in Serving Community (De Pree, 1997).

Our perspectives on leadership have matured a great deal over the last century. We have progressed all the way from the belief that leaders are born, not made, to embracing the notion that leaders must connect with all others in an organization in such a way that the organization becomes a reflection of common core values that serve to raise the organization to a higher moral and ethical level. That's quite a journey by any stretch of the imagination!

Caring Enough to Lead seeks to expand the discussion of leadership further to get at what it really means to be a leader. As Sergiovanni (1992) so succinctly points out,

> The management values now considered legitimate are biased toward rationality, logic, objectivity, the importance of self-interest, explicitness, individuality, and detachment. *Emphasizing* these values causes us to *neglect* emotions, the importance of group membership, sense and meaning, morality, self-sacrifice, duty, and obligation as *additional* values.
>
> Furthermore, the bases of authority for today's leadership practice rely heavily on bureaucracy, psychological knowledge or skill, and the technical rationality that emerges from theory and research. *Emphasizing* those three bases causes us to *neglect* professional and moral authority as *additional* bases for leadership practice. (p. xiii)

In the simplest terms, this book is not concerned with what leaders say, know, or are able to do. All these elements of leadership have been dealt with sufficiently in the past. *Caring Enough to Lead* is about *being* a leader. I firmly believe that Sergiovanni (1992) is correct in his contention that we have viewed leadership from a narrow perspective in the past. In doing so, we may have negated what could be the most important aspects of what it means to be a leader, the so-called moral dimension of leadership. *Caring Enough to Lead* is a deliberate attempt to understand and expand some of the yet unexplored and heretofore unexplained dimensions of moral leadership.

Intended Audience

Caring Enough to Lead has several intended audiences. This book is not just for principals or other administrative personnel, present or future, but for all those who feel a deep personal responsibility, a sacred trust, to provide the most effective leadership they can in whatever roles they may find themselves serving. Therefore, the content of this book is appropriate for a broad range of educational professionals, including teachers, principals, guidance counselors, media specialists, coaches, nurses, psychologists, superintendents, school board members, and just about anyone else committed to being the best leader he or she can be while helping colleagues realize this same goal. The book is intended for both practicing educational professionals as well as those in the process of preparing for a career in the field of education. My hope in writing *Caring Enough to Lead* is to help those with leadership responsibilities understand that leading is concerned much more with *being* than it is with *knowing* and *doing!* And caring is at the very center of being.

Unique Features of the Book

The content of this book is based on my nearly thirty-five years of experience as a professional educator in a variety of leadership roles. The fundamental truths that are the gist of this discussion of leadership are based on real-life experiences rather than expert opinion. The majority of the chapter titles are in the form of questions, and many additional questions are included in the text to help the reader focus on fundamental elements of successful leadership (e.g., What do I care about? What do I believe about people?). Scenarios, metaphors, and vignettes are used to illustrate key points and make the reading of the book an enjoyable and enlightening personal experience rather than just another academic exercise. A special feature of this revision of *Caring Enough to Lead* is the inclusion of a set of reflective exercises at the end of each chapter. These exercises encourage readers to step back and examine in a very personal way who they are as leaders and as human beings and who they want to become. By completing these reflective exercises, readers can produce personal "journals" documenting their individual journeys to becoming the kind of leaders that they want to be.

Need for the Book

Two centuries ago, Thomas Jefferson warned that a nation could not expect to be both free and ignorant at the same time. The demands of citizenship in a democratic society are simply too great to allow freedom and ignorance to exist on the same plane. Jefferson's warning is as relevant today as it was at the birth of our nation. We must continually strive to do our best as a democratic society to educate all our citizens to assume the responsibilities and enjoy the freedoms of citizenship. To do less represents a moral failure on the part of society. Our schools have never needed excellent leadership more than they do today. They are under attack from every quarter. The problems facing society have never been greater, and the importance of a highly educated citizenry to help solve those problems has never been more critical.

The longer I live, the more I realize the important role that education plays in the quality of the life that one is permitted to live. Looking back over more than five decades, I am more aware than ever that almost everything that I have done, will do, am presently, or ever will be can be attributed to the quality of the education that I have been fortunate enough to receive. It's nothing short of amazing when I think about it: Almost everything in my life, both large and small, I can directly or indirectly attribute to my education. For example, the job that I have, the car that I drive, the house that I live in, the woman I am married to, the friends that I have, the places I've traveled, even the things that interest me, and the things that I like and dislike, can all be connected in one way or another to the education that I have received. Even the thoughts that I think, the things that I value, and the things that I believe—much of what I would regard as my basic humanity—I can attribute to the quality of my education.

Education is indeed the cornerstone of a democracy, and the quality of education available to all the citizens in a democracy is a barometer of the level of caring on the part of one human being for another that exists in a society. In my view, we are experiencing a crisis in caring in America, a crisis that prevents us from doing all that we can to educate all the citizens of this country effectively. The single greatest problem we are facing in American education today is that we lack the will as a society to do what we know how to do, and can do, to educate all the children of this nation effectively. Sometimes I fear that we have become so self-absorbed as individuals and as a nation that we longer care enough about the education of our fellow citizens!

The problem resulting from a lack of caring is not a problem that you can solve with your head, it's a problem that you must solve with your heart. This book is written for those who have the heart to care enough to lead; it is especially for those who want to help others care enough to provide the critical leadership needed to solve the fundamental problems afflicting American education.

Scope and Treatment

Caring Enough to Lead is a collection of ideas and understandings rather than a "how-to" manual. The chapters, which are relatively brief, illustrate important concepts of leadership through a series of questions, short vignettes, selected quotations, and personal stories. Although the first and last chapters need to appear in that order, most of the others could easily be placed at random because they are self-contained and complete wherever they occur in the book. Below are brief descriptions of the contents of several selected chapters to illustrate the uniqueness of the book.

Chapter 1, "It's Better to Know Some of the Questions Than All the Answers," sets the stage for the chapters that follow. The essence of this chapter is that questions are more important than answers for leaders because life's essential questions are eternal, whereas answers to questions frequently vary with time, circumstances, and personalities. Because questions are more important than answers for leaders, the remainder of the book suggests some of the essential questions that leaders should be asking and answering for themselves if they hope to be able to lead effectively.

Chapter 4, "What Do I Care About?" illustrates that the essential things that a person cares about determine to a great extent who that person is as a human being and as a leader. The question, "What do I care about?" is critical for school leaders, because the things that a person values most highly will dictate what he or she will be passionate about, will fight for, sacrifice for, and in extreme cases, even die for if necessary.

Chapter 5, "What Do I Believe About People?" asks the reader to take the time to examine his or her personal point of reference in dealing with professional colleagues. I describe my basic four-part, personal personnel philosophy as an example of an orientation to working with others to help them succeed, and in turn help the organization to succeed.

Chapter 10, "Am I Taking Care of My Water Buffalo?" is concerned with the role that cooperation and understanding can play in successful leadership. The story of a farmer and a water buffalo plowing a rice paddy together is used to illustrate how much we need each other to accomplish any worthwhile goal. The point is made that although there are many different roles to play in any organization, every role is critical to the success or failure of the organization.

Chapter 16, "Can I Care Enough to Be My Own Best Friend?" deals with the essential mind-set required to treasure oneself as one does a dear friend. Leadership roles are demanding and stressful. This chapter discusses the importance of taking care of oneself in a leadership role and offers suggestions for self-renewal and for dealing with the stresses and strains associated with leadership roles.

Chapter 21, "Your Leadership Becomes You!" is the final chapter and describes the metamorphosis that one must experience to become a leader. One becomes a leader by discovering personal answers to the questions posed in the preceding chapters. This chapter emphasizes that being a leader is not something one does—rather, it is something one becomes.

Acknowledgments

There have been precious few times in my life when I have been afforded the opportunity to write something that I genuinely wanted to write. This book is the exception. I am eternally grateful to Corwin Press for giving me this opportunity to write something that I really wanted to write. Robb, what a genuine pleasure it was to work with you as my editor. No editor could have been more responsive to my inquiries or conscientious while considering my proposals. Over the past few months, I have come to realize that you truly have a gift for sensing what works and what doesn't. Carla, thank you for doing such a wonderful job of editing the copy. You certainly demonstrated a great deal of caring by going far beyond what was required in order to do the job in an exemplary manner. To my role models, Aretha, Barbara, Ken, Peggy, Rudolph, Sandy, and Tom, thank you for showing me what it means to be a leader. I also want to thank those who read drafts and offered advice during the writing of this book, especially Deborah Z. Waldron, Thomas Gannon, and Susan Fortune. Their contributions as reviewers are gratefully acknowledged. I am especially grateful to my graduate students who made all those trips to the library, checked my references for me, and helped me find stuff when I lost it. Thank you! Thank you! Thank you! Ginny, Thelma, Phyllis, and Megan. Finally, I want to thank all my colleagues with whom I have worked at the University of South Carolina and the University of La Verne. What an honor and a privilege it has been for me to have been a part of such a dedicated and caring group of educational leaders for most of my professional life.

Corwin Press gratefully acknowledge the contributions of the following reviewers:

Dr. Mary K. McCullough
Coordinator, Administrative Services
School of Education, Loyola Marymount University
Los Angeles, CA

Doug Roby
Assistant Professor of Educational Leadership
Wright State University
Dayton, OH

Dr. David A. Steele
Professional Development Services
School of Education, Seattle Pacific University
Seattle, WA

About the Author

 **Leonard O. Pellicer** is Dean of the School of Education and Organizational Leadership at the University of La Verne and Distinguished Professor Emeritus from the University of South Carolina. He has served in a number of teaching and leadership roles over the past thirty-five years. He served as the first director of the South Carolina Educational Policy Center, at the University of South Carolina, and was also the director of the African American Professors Program, a program designed to address the problem of a shortage of African American professors at predominantly white higher-education institutions. His experiences prior to joining the faculty at the University of South Carolina include service as a high school and middle school teacher, high school assistant principal, high school principal, and director of a teacher education center that provided staff development opportunities for teachers and administrators in five Florida school districts. From 1986 to 1987, he was a Fulbright Scholar in Southeast Asia. During this period, he taught graduate classes at the University of the Philippines and used his expertise in school leadership to assist in developing programs to train school leaders in the region. From 1992 to 1995, he spent a good

deal of time in the Republic of South Africa as a member of a team that developed a field-based training program for black principals in the "new South Africa." He holds a bachelor's degree in English education and master's and doctoral degrees in educational administration from the University of Florida in Gainesville. For more than twenty-five years, he has written, consulted, and spoken extensively in the areas of school leadership, instructional leadership, and educational programs for disadvantaged students. He has coauthored two other books with Lorin Anderson for Corwin Press, including *A Handbook for Teacher Leaders* (1995) and *Teacher Peer Assistance and Review: A Practical Guide for Teachers and Administrators* (2001).

It's Better to Know Some of the Questions Than All the Answers

I enjoy mowing my grass on Saturday mornings. I'm not sure why this is such a pleasurable experience for me, but it really and truly is something I look forward to doing. One of the things I enjoy most is the smell of the newly mowed grass; another is the feeling of accomplishment that comes with completing a project that allows you to admire the results of your labor instantly. Those of us who are educators never tire of experiences like this, experiences that provide even a small measure of instant gratification. Maybe this is because it seems as if we have to wait most of a lifetime to see the results of our efforts with children in classrooms.

Although I like smelling the newly mowed grass and admiring the results of my handiwork, perhaps the thing I like best about mowing my grass is the feeling of power I derive from mowing down all those thousands and thousands of blades of grass while gliding along effortlessly behind my almost new, Honda self-propelled mower. When I first brought my Honda mower home from the store, my wife took one look at it and exclaimed, "Wow! It looks like you could drive it to town." My wife doesn't exaggerate—it's an impressive mower!

Over the years, I have established a pattern for mowing my grass that suits me perfectly. I always begin by cutting all the odd-shaped, uneven areas around the edges of my yard first so that after a while, I'm left with a large circle of uncut grass in the middle of the yard. Then I go round and round the circle in a nice easy rhythm interrupted only by my stopping occasionally to empty the bulging grass bag. It's downright peaceful!

As I cruise along effortlessly, watching the circle grow smaller and smaller with each completed circuit, I wear my genuine "Dale Earnhardt" earphones and listen to public radio.

There are a lot of good shows on PBS radio on Saturday mornings. There's "Car Talk" and "Rabbit Ears Radio" and my favorite mowing show, "What Do You Know?" which sounds like "Whadda Ya Know?" when you hear it on the radio. "Whadda Ya Know?" is produced by Public Radio International and is broadcast out of Wisconsin. The host of the show is the clever and entertaining Michael Feldman. Michael always begins the show with a question for his live and listening radio audiences. "Whadda ya know?" he asks in a rather loud and demanding voice, to which the members of the studio audience (and all of us listening out there in radio land as well) reply in unison, "Not much!"

The show is a quiz show, and as it progresses, it becomes more and more evident that the contestants on the show don't, in fact, know very much.

At least they don't know very much about the questions that Michael Feldman has for them. The questions on the show are designed to cross up the contestants and make them look foolish by asking about silly and often obscure facts gleaned from nonsensical categories, such as "Things you should have learned in school had you been paying attention." The producers of "Whadda Ya Know?" acknowledge that the questions are a little ridiculous with a disclaimer that advises the listeners to get their own shows if they don't like the questions used on "Whadda Ya Know?"

Twenty-five years ago, had you asked me "Whadda ya know?" I would have responded differently to the question than I would now. Like many young people (including the two sons that grew up in my house over the past two decades), I thought I knew just about everything in this world that I needed to know. It was during this early period of "self-enlightenment" that I was asked by my state school administrators association to deliver a series of workshops at a number of locations around the state. The purpose of the workshops was to help building-level school administrators improve their skills as instructional leaders. Now, I must tell you that I feel strongly about the importance of instructional leadership in schools. But I must also tell you that I have a problem with discussing this topic in public. It seems that I have a predisposition to preach on any topic about which I care deeply—unfortunately, that includes a fairly broad range of topics, because I am a very caring person. At any rate, if I'm not extremely vigilant, suddenly, and without warning, I can find myself preaching rather than teaching.

Apparently, that's exactly what happened to me when I delivered my series of workshops on instructional leadership those many years ago. I was sitting in my office one day after the series had concluded, congratulating myself on the fine job I had done, when I received a piece of correspondence in the mail.

The message was simple and straightforward. The message read, "It's better to know some of the questions than all the answers!" Below this simple message was the inscription, "James Thurber (1894–1961)." At first I was flattered; I thought James Thurber had sent me the message. But almost instantly, reality set in, and I realized that James couldn't have sent me the message, because he had been dead for quite some time before someone used his words of wisdom to pull me down off of my pedestal and plunk me firmly back down on the ground where I belonged. I had been so busy telling everyone the answers to becoming an instructional leader that I had forgotten the most essential questions.

To this day, I have no idea who sent me that simple but powerful message. At first, I was offended at the implied put-down, but after I'd thought about it for awhile, I was grateful. Whoever that thoughtful and caring person was who sent me the message, I want to thank him or her for reminding me that I should be focusing more on the essential questions in my life and not worrying so much about the answers. For although the answers to life's most important questions may vary with the times, with a particular set of circumstances that exists at a given time, or with the persons who are doing the asking or being asked the questions, the essential questions remain eternal.

In her wonderful book, *Leadership and the New Science*, Margaret J. Wheatley (1992) says this about the uncertain nature of life and the futility of wanting someone else to give us the answers to life's most important questions:

> I haven't stopped wanting someone, somewhere to return with the right answers. But I know that my hopes are old, based on a different universe. In this new world, you and I make it up as we go along, not because we lack expertise or planning skills, but because that is the nature of reality. Reality changes shape and meaning because of our activity. And it is constantly new. We are required to be there, as active participants. It can't happen without us and nobody can do it for us. (p. 151)

I believe (and I don't mean to be preaching here) that the very best leaders spend a great deal more time pondering the important questions in life than they do dispensing the "correct" answers. It's not the right or even the responsibility of a leader always to have the right answers to life's most important questions. It is, however, the responsibility of a leader to acknowledge that these crucial questions exist for every organization and every individual within an organization. Realizing the transitory nature of human experiences in organizations, it is the responsibility of a leader to work faithfully with others in the organization to seek the answers to the questions most relevant to them at a particular time under a prevailing set of circumstances. Ultimately, struggling together with the critical questions will do more to define a successful organization than all the answers in the world. In my view, asking the critical questions in the right ways at the appropriate times helps to define one who is caring enough to lead. Therefore, in the chapters that follow, we will have plenty of opportunities to ponder important questions together. As we embark on our mutual journey, I want to prime you with a single question: Whadda ya know?

Why Am I Going to Visit Bob?

A wonderful friend and colleague recently died of Alzheimer's disease. My friend Bob and I had worked together for more than fifteen years at the University of South Carolina, and we remained good friends even after his retirement from the university several years ago. For all of you who never had the pleasure of knowing Bob, I can tell you with a high degree of certainty that he was just the kind of guy you'd really enjoy spending a little time with. Bob had that special kind of wisdom about him that comes from living a long, thoughtful, and caring kind of life. He was exceedingly kind, generous to a fault, and had a genuine zest for living. Had Bob been raised in the South, I would have declared him a true southern gentleman, because he exuded the manners, grace, and style of that rare and dying breed. One of the things I liked most about Bob was his unusually well-developed sense of humor; he truly loved to laugh. I honestly don't believe that I ever spent more than five or ten minutes with Bob that we didn't laugh together at least once. Whenever I needed a lift, I would seek him out, and he never disappointed. I would always leave his presence feeling a little less anxious about my present circumstances and decidedly more optimistic about my future prospects.

It was shocking to me how quickly the disease ravaged Bob's mind, body, and personality. I had what I thought was a normal conversation with him on the telephone one day in June. But by August of that same year, his beautiful wife of more than fifty years, Barbara, called me in tears to let me know that she had had to place Bob in a care facility because she was no longer able to adequately care for him in their home.

After Bob was institutionalized, I visited him whenever I was near the area where the care facility was located. At first, his physical appearance was about the same as it had always been, and we had nice chats about people, places, and experiences that we had shared over the years. We still laughed together a good bit, although I'm not absolutely certain we were always laughing at the same things. But that didn't matter at the time. All that mattered was that we enjoyed the visits and had fun together. Sadly, as the weeks and months passed, Bob's physical appearance began to change, the light in his eyes grew dimmer, and little by little, he lost touch with reality until he was no longer able to communicate effectively with the outside world.

The last time I visited with Bob, his physical appearance was so altered that I wouldn't have known who he was had I not witnessed the remarkable transformation at short intervals. By this time, the only sounds Bob could make were mostly unintelligible to everyone except Barbara. Bob and Barbara, much like some identical twins, still seemed to share a secret language that allowed them to stay in close touch with each other despite the relentless advancement of the disease. Although I could no longer understand the sounds that came from Bob when he attempted to speak, I still pretended that I knew what he was trying to communicate to me. I gave a little laugh or inserted a "Yeah, I know" into the conversation at what I estimated to be the most appropriate points. All the while, Barbara continued to assure me that Bob knew who I was and that he was very glad to see me.

In July of 2000, I moved from South Carolina to California, to accept a new job opportunity. After the move west, I returned periodically to the East Coast for various reasons, and I always made it a point to go by the care facility to spend a little time with Bob and Barbara. Each time, I would telephone Barbara ahead to let her know when I was going to see Bob so that the three of us could visit together. It meant so much to Barbara that some of Bob's friends and colleagues still spent a little time with him, especially as his illness progressed. I think that Barbara felt that the visits with friends and colleagues restored a little dignity to Bob, by somehow acknowledging that this wonderful human being still existed somewhere inside that spent body confined to the wheelchair.

One of the last times I was scheduled to visit with Bob and Barbara, I had spent the morning with another friend and former colleague of Bob's and was running a little behind schedule. I glanced at my watch and told my friend that I had to get going or I would be late for my visit with Bob. He didn't bother masking the surprised look on his face as he asked, "Why are you going to visit Bob? You know his disease has progressed to the point that he's not even going to know who you are." "I suppose you're right," I replied in what probably sounded like an apologetic tone. But then I was quick to add, "He probably won't know who I am, but Barbara will, and it's important to her that people still care enough about Bob to come and spend some time with him. I suppose that at this point, I'm visiting Bob more for Barbara's sake than I am for Bob's." My friend nodded his acceptance of this line of reasoning as I hurried to my car.

When I arrived for my visit, Bob, Barbara, and I sat together in the large family room of the care facility with about fifteen other Alzheimer's patients. Out of the corner of my eye, I noticed a tiny, silver-haired woman sitting in a wheelchair, watching us closely from the far side of the room. As Barbara and I talked about items of common interest and Bob occasionally added his own unique input to the conversation, I noticed that the old woman in the wheelchair was slowly moving closer and closer to where the three of us were sitting.

She shuffled her feet almost imperceptibly, and inch by inch, she drew nearer to us. After a time, she was positioned directly behind me in her wheelchair. Then suddenly, without warning, she slid her arm through an opening in the back of the chair in which I was sitting, placed her hand squarely on top of my hand, and leaned her head against the back of my right shoulder! I didn't know exactly what I should say or do, but it was very clear to me that this woman was desperately in need of a little human contact. So I placed my other hand on top of hers, and we remained locked together in that unusual embrace for the rest of my visit with Bob and Barbara.

After the visit was over, and I was walking across the parking lot of the care facility to my car, I thought about Bob's illness, my periodic visits over the past couple of years, and what it all meant. At that moment, I came to the conclusion that I wasn't visiting Bob just for Bob's sake—most likely, he didn't know, and he probably didn't even care who I was at that point in his life. I also realized that I wasn't visiting Bob just for Barbara's sake. Although I sensed that my visits were extremely important to her, and I genuinely wanted to help ease her burden, I wasn't visiting her husband just to satisfy her needs. No! That definitely wasn't it! I wasn't there primarily for Bob or for Barbara. The honest truth is that I was there for me!

I was there because I want to be the kind of person who continues to care about his friends and colleagues even after they are no longer capable of returning that caring in kind. I want to be the kind of person who has the capacity to give without expecting anything in return. I want to be the kind of person who is sensitive to the needs of others and caring enough to want to meet those needs in the best way that I can. You see, my being there was tangible evidence for me that I am becoming more like the person that I ultimately want to be. Although anyone who knows me well will tell you that I have a long way to go on the journey to becoming that kind of person, it was somehow comforting for me at that precise moment to know that I was at least moving in the right direction. I would wager most of us don't get these kinds of confirmations nearly as often as we would like in our everyday lives, so when we do, they are very special moments indeed. These moments act as signposts to let us know that we are on our chosen paths toward becoming the person that we want to be.

Now that Bob has passed away and I am looking back on these experiences, I realize more than ever that Bob and Barbara were not the primary beneficiaries of my visits. *I was the primary beneficiary!* After nearly sixty years of living, I have come to believe that the only real joy in life comes from living a life that matters. People live lives that matter by doing meaningful things for others. Visiting Bob gave me a golden opportunity to demonstrate to myself that I genuinely cared enough to do something meaningful for my friend. Consequently, visiting Bob gave me great joy. In the end, I came to realize that this was Bob's gift to me.

By this time, you are probably wondering, "What in the world does all this have to do with leadership?" My reply is a very simple one: "Going to visit Bob has everything to do with leadership!" It has everything to do with leadership because every one of us is on the way to visit Bob. Regardless of who we are, each of us is inexorably moving along on our individual life's journey toward becoming the friend, student, parent, lover, colleague, spouse, leader, and ultimately, the human being that we want to be. Nobody can choose the best paths for us to follow on this journey; we have to choose our own paths. Occasionally, there will be times when we race ahead, sure that we are going in the right direction. There will also be times when we will stumble and fall, and still other times when we become so totally disoriented that we will temporarily lose our way. All the while, however, we must remember that it's all about the journey, not the destination. We have to be patient and look out for the signposts (such as the one that Bob gave to me) along the way to reassure us that we are, after all, moving in the right direction. In the future, should someone ask me, "Why are you going to visit Bob?" surely I will have a much better answer. How about you?

In the chapters to follow, I will suggest some signposts for you in the form of critical questions and brief exercises. I sincerely hope that you will take the time to consider the questions and complete the exercises. Perhaps in this way, you will be able to create a sort of personal journal to help document precisely where you are on the path that you have chosen on your journey to becoming the leader and human being you want to be.

Take Time to Reflect

Take a minute to reflect, and see if you can recall a recent event in your life that confirmed for you that you were on the right path to becoming the kind of leader/person that you want to be.

What was the event, and what special insight did you gain from this experience in terms of who you are becoming as a leader and a person?

_____

_____

_____

_____

_____

_____

_____

_____

_____

_____

_____

_____

_____

What Is a Leader?

I have been blessed many times in my life. One of my most cherished blessings is that I was fortunate enough to be born in a community situated directly beside the Atlantic Ocean. As I write this, it's early March, and I'm back in my hometown for a few days, ensconced in a seaside beach home belonging to a couple of my oldest and dearest friends. After nearly a week of rain and cold weather, this morning broke as a bright and beautiful spring day. From time to time, I can't resist ceasing my labors and looking out the window toward the ocean. There's a gentle but steady northeaster blowing across the magnificent landscape. Each time I look up from my work, the sea oats are waving to me, beckoning me to come out and play. The golden sun is streaming down on the blue-green surf, which is pounding out a steady rhythm against the gleaming white sand, while squadrons of pelicans fly by in their V-shaped formations as if on some secret search-and-destroy mission. It takes all the self-control I can muster to resist the sea oats and the sand and the surf and the pelicans. But I need to be strong this morning. I must direct all my energy toward exploring a difficult question, the answer to which has eluded countless others far more enlightened than me for centuries. The question I am referring to is, "What is a leader?"

More than 35 years ago, I was happy to be back in this small seaside city where I spent my youth. I had returned to my hometown on leave from active duty in the navy. It was the early 1960s. The Vietnam War was heating up, and the air squadron in which I served had just returned to the United States after a year-long cruise aboard an aircraft carrier in the South China Sea. When you're nineteen or twenty years old, a year out of your life is a long time indeed. I felt as if I had been away forever. I couldn't wait to get back to my roots; I was desperate to touch base with my high school buddies and to get back down on the beach, where I could feel I was at long last home again.

As soon as I arrived at my parents' home, I got on the phone and started calling all my old friends around town, hoping to catch up on everything I had missed during the eternity that I had been away. As luck would have it, one of my best friends was just leaving his house with his fiancée to go for a ride on the beach in his jeep. He invited me to ride along.

A strong northeaster had been pummeling the coast for several days. The powerful wind and the wild surf made for an exciting and highly entertaining afternoon for the three of us in the jeep. We saw all kinds of interesting things as we rode up and down and over and around the sand dunes. There were fat, green, slimy mounds of seaweed; a virtual fortune in sand dollars; lots of pointy, brown starfish; a variety of colorful and unusual seashells; and even a dead porpoise that had washed up among the collage of sea artifacts displayed along the shore. As we rounded the jetties that protected the inlet into the harbor at the north end of the beach, we were surprised to see a shrimp boat that had grounded itself on the rocks and been abandoned about 100 yards offshore. The punishing winds and driving currents had succeeded in dismantling a portion of the outer shell of the boat; some of the planks had already washed up on the beach by the time we arrived on the scene. We paused in our journey for some time to speculate on what might have caused the boat to founder, and we wondered out loud about the fate of the crew who had been on board.

It was at this juncture that we saw something we had never seen before in all our many years of exploring the beach: a huge dead octopus blown ashore by the strong winds. The octopus formed a large gray lump on the smooth white surface of the beach, even though it was partially buried by the wet sand. The sight was so unusual that it compelled the three of us to get out of the jeep and conduct a closer inspection. We poked and prodded the dead creature with sticks and stretched it out until it extended over a diameter of six to eight feet. We were all pretty excited by the find, but my friend's fiancée was beside herself with amazement. When she saw the strange animal fully extended, she exclaimed, "My God—would you look at those huge testicles!" While futilely struggling to repress his laughter, my friend quickly corrected his betrothed, "Tentacles, Honey! Tentacles!" he said.

The young woman made a humorous but common mistake, a mistake that is unremarkable to all of us as we seek to understand and explain to others the range of mysterious and wonderful things that we encounter in our everyday lives. Frequently, when we encounter something that we aren't familiar with or that we don't fully understand, initially we may not even know what we're looking at! Even if we do know what we're looking at, we may not know what to call it! In many ways, leadership is an octopus. It's much easier to recognize it when we see it than it is to understand it or to explain it to others.

That being said, let us briefly explore together some of the characteristics and qualities of leadership from the perspectives of some of those who have studied it, written about it, experienced it, or practiced it. Together, we will poke it and prod it a bit. If we're lucky, maybe we'll even be able to spread out its tentacles until we can make a faint outline of this thing called leadership.

Most of us are familiar with the routine dictionary-type definitions of leadership that talk about leaders as special people who somehow get things done through others or as those who have the skills to move a group of people toward a common goal, to take people in a direction that they may not otherwise have chosen to go. These kinds of definitions are quite common and have been around forever. Based on a review of a series of leadership studies, Hogan, Curphy, and Hogan (1994) suggest, for example, that "leadership involves persuading other people to set aside for a period of time their individual concerns and to pursue a common goal that is important for the responsibilities and welfare of a group" (p. 493). The key to a leader's effectiveness, according to these writers, is "his or her ability to build a team" (p. 499) to get things done. Although most of us would agree that leaders are able to get things done in one way or another, such definitions don't shed much light on the essential nature of leadership.

Some of the more recent definitions of leadership are perhaps more useful in that they focus more on what leaders *are* rather than what they are able to *do.* For example, Sergiovanni (1992) says that "The heart of leadership has to do with what a person believes, values, dreams about, and is committed to—the person's *personal vision,* to use the popular term" (p. 7).

Sergiovanni (1992) describes leaders as the first followers in the sense that "followership requires an emotional commitment to a set of ideas" (p. 71). As he points out, "Hierarchical position and personality are not enough to earn one the mantle of leader. Instead, it comes through one's demonstrated devotion and success as a follower. The true leader is the one who follows first" (p. 72).

By linking the importance of beliefs, values, and dreams to leadership behaviors, Sergiovanni (1992) stresses the importance of joining the heart and the head of leadership with the hand of leadership. In this way, leaders become authentic to those who are inspired to follow them, because the things that leaders do reflect what both the leaders and the followers think, feel, and believe. In this way, a leader's actions, decisions, and behaviors can more easily be understood, respected, and appreciated by those who follow, resulting in a covenantal community that is more sacred in its nature than it is secular.

Max De Pree (1989), the noted management expert and former CEO of Herman Miller, one of the most successful corporate entities in the world, expresses the belief that leadership is not a science, but more of an art: "Leadership is much more an art, a belief, a condition of the heart, than a set of things to do" (p. 148). To De Pree, being a leader requires liberating people in an organizational setting, "to do what is required of them in the most effective and humane way possible" (p. 1). Leaders are servants to their followers in that they seek to remove the obstacles that prevent them from doing their jobs and to give them the freedom and incentive to live up to their potential, while completing themselves as human beings. In De Pree's words, "The first responsibility of a leader is to define reality. The last is to say thank you. In between the two, the leader must become a servant and a debtor" (p. 11). According to De Pree, "Leaders owe the organization a new reference point for what caring, purposeful, committed people can be in an institutional setting" (p. 15). They must help to define a set of clear organizational values, encourage contrary opinions, provide joy, respect all individuals, communicate effectively, and in every way possible, take full advantage of the opportunities that leadership provides to "make a meaningful difference in the lives of those who permit leaders to lead" (p. 22). Like Sergiovanni (1992), De Pree believes that effective leadership ultimately depends on a covenantal relationship between leaders and followers based on a common core of shared values.

Walt Tobin, who has been selected Superintendent of the Year on several occasions by various organizations and has served as president of the superintendent's association in South Carolina, has described leadership in terms of what he calls "soft skills." If you ask his opinion about what makes some leaders better than others, he can rattle off a laundry list of attributes such as integrity, trust, dependability, fairness, honesty, dignity, and visibility. These attributes have little to do with what a leader knows or even does, but a lot to do with the kind of human being the leader is. Tobin says that leaders must find out what's important to others and then make it important to themselves. He suggests that leaders must be willing to "color outside the lines" and remain as calm and focused as officials on a basketball court, even though things are happening fast and furiously all around them. Referring to a recent furor in his school district related to a legislatively mandated consolidation of several smaller rural school districts with his own, Tobin joked about the high degree of uncertainty that leaders must deal with routinely: "I thought I would take this old gray mare (his school district) and ride it into the sunset—suddenly, this sucker decided to gallop on me!"

Aside from all the tools required for successful leadership, however, Tobin feels that successful leaders are able to find joy in what they're doing. As he put it, "After more than thirty years, I still love to hear a first grader read."

Michele Forman, 2001 National Teacher of the Year and an outstanding teacher leader, has defined teacher leadership as follows:

> Teacher leadership means first of all staying focused on students and their learning. Student learning is the reason schools exist and teachers teach. A teacher leader models excellence in teaching and understands the extraordinary potential of each learner, the tentative nature of knowledge, and the necessity of continuous growth and renewal as a professional. . . . True leaders reject hierarchy and value others' abilities and contributions. They celebrate the creativity and the challenge of good teaching and exhibit enormous reserves of intellectual, emotional, and physical energy that fuel their own growth, even as they nurture their students and support their colleagues. . . . Teacher leaders appreciate the importance and dignity of their work. They know they make a difference. (Personal communication, October 25, 2002)

When asked to give her views on the essential elements of effective leadership, Cynthia Cervantes McGuire, who has almost two decades of successful experience as an elementary school principal and was chosen to receive her school district's initial Manager of the Year award, described leadership as "giving—it's knowing who you are and keeping in touch with your core; it's making mistakes, failing, and succeeding. . . . Leadership is following, it's having spirit and soul. It's giving back tenfold what was given you." Cervantes McGuire regards leadership as "a journey through uncharted waters" requiring "guts and courage." Most important, however, she feels that leadership is "about staying in love with what you do."

You can feel Cervantes McGuire's love for serving others in these comments she made as she accepted her award as Manager of the Year:

> There are times, as I'm rising early in the morning, that I lament the fact that I've not yet won the lottery. And then as I get closer to my exit on the 210 freeway, I take great comfort in the recognition that I do have riches untold. I work with people—colleagues and community—that I consider friends and family. I work with people of uncommon spirit and unending purpose. I am rich!

That love is also generously reflected in the voices of those Cervantes McGuire works with on a daily basis. After all, who is better qualified to judge a person's leadership than the recipients of it? Below are excerpts from several of the letters written in support of Cervantes McGuire's nomination as Manager of the Year in the Azusa, California, Unified School District, by those who have been touched by her leadership:

> Thank you Mrs. Cervantes McGuire for being the kind of person that a parent would choose to care for her children. . . . You make the time to spend with students and really listen to them. . . . You have set goals and

standards, implemented programs, and coalesced the staff into a truly remarkable teaching team sharing the common goal of always striving to provide the best for children. . . . I am so pleased and honored to have the privilege of knowing you, and to have you in my children's lives. (School site council member and parent)

I have been touched by the many gifts Cynthia brings to and shares in her work. . . . Cynthia has a gift for making each staff member feel valued and vital to our school community. Cynthia's thoughts, concerns, and actions always represent the deep commitment which she has to the lives of students as well as staff. Cynthia navigates the roles of manager and friend very well. At times I am not sure who is supporting me, Cynthia the manager or Cynthia the friend. It is this personal quality of her leadership that I admire and value most. She is a beacon of encouragement with whom I am honored and blessed to work so closely. (First-year teacher)

A good leader is one who has an open mind, a compassionate heart, and a willingness to listen. . . . Cynthia has all those qualities and much more! When asking opinions or thoughts from employees, students, and parents, her consideration is sincere—never undermining of one's position. Cynthia has the ability to make us all feel important and valued as instructional aides and parents, but more important, as people. (Parent and instructional aide)

In all these statements of support, one sees a common thread of love and genuine caring reflected back from the recipients of Cervantes McGuire's leadership, regardless of their roles in the school community. One sees a confirmation of Sergiovanni's (1992) and De Pree's (1989) concept of moral leadership in an organization that is nurtured and sustained by a common set of beliefs, values, and dreams that have helped to create an organization that is more like a family than it is a public institution. Clearly, a covenant existed among all the members of this particular school community. It is little wonder that Cervantes McGuire was singled out for her leadership or that her school was designated as a distinguished school by the State of California. As another veteran teacher noted in her letter of support, "Our school is now a vibrant and exciting place to be. To me, Cynthia is the manager of the millennium rather than the year!"

A dear friend and colleague recently went to visit her daughter in Atlanta. Her daughter had purchased a new home and invited her mother to come and see her new place. It was arranged that the daughter would meet my friend on the edge of town and guide the way. The two met as planned, and the daughter took the lead and pulled out into heavy rush-hour traffic on the expressway. My friend told me how her daughter drove in and out of the traffic at increasingly higher rates of speed. At first, her daughter was going fifty miles per hour, then sixty and seventy, and finally eighty! My friend became more and more concerned as she tried in vain to keep up with her speeding daughter.

Suddenly, my friend realized that she was foolish to try to follow behind in heavy traffic at such excessive speeds. As my friend put it, "My daughter is twenty-five years old—she has a right to be foolish. But I'm fifty! Why was I risking my life in rush-hour traffic on an expressway in Atlanta?" As soon as my friend came to this realization, she pulled off the expressway at the next exit, went to a nearby shopping mall, and spent the next several hours shopping. When she felt her daughter had had sufficient time to agonize over her whereabouts, my friend called her from a pay phone and told her where she was. When the relieved young woman arrived at the mall to retrieve her mother, my friend had some carefully chosen words for her:

> I was in a vulnerable situation not being acquainted with how to get to your house in the unfamiliar, rush-hour traffic. I trusted you to lead me, but you didn't

care enough to maintain close contact with me. You went on your own merry way without so much as a backward glance to see if I was following or if I needed your help. When I became convinced that you weren't concerned about me and my needs, I made a decision to stop following you. Do you think that you are now able to lead me to your home in a responsible and caring way?

Needless to say, the daughter was a caring and considerate leader as she guided her mother from the mall parking lot to her home. She checked her rearview mirror frequently and adjusted her speed to make sure that she never again lost contact with her mother. In due time, they both arrived safely at their destination.

There is a valuable lesson in this little story for all who desire to lead. Leadership requires a high level of care and concern on the part of the leader for those who would choose to follow. Whenever a leader fails to exercise the level of care and concern required to maintain close contact with his or her followers, the implied contract between the leader and followers is voided. Contrary to popular opinion, true leaders are never really out in front of others, as we so often hear people say they are. Rather, the best leaders are precisely in the middle of the beliefs, dreams, and values of those whom they lead. Permission to lead can come only through the consent of those who willingly give up their right to go off in their own directions in favor of going in the group's direction. As they move forward, leaders must constantly look to their left and to their right and occasionally behind them to make sure that they are still in the center of the group. The moment they lose contact with the beliefs and goals and dreams of the group, they lose their capacity to lead.

A couple of years ago, I had the good fortune to be seated next to James MacGregor Burns at a luncheon. Burns is regarded by many as the foremost presidential scholar who ever lived, and his book, so simply titled *Leadership* (1978), won both the Pulitzer Prize and a National Book Award. Naturally, I took advantage of the fortuitous circumstance provided by our close proximity to question Burns about some of his ideas on leadership. I had read his book, and I knew how he had defined leadership in his writing. I knew, for example, that he regarded power and leadership as separate entities: "Power wielders may treat people as things. Leaders may not. All leaders are actual or potential power holders, but not all power holders are leaders" (p. 18). I also knew that Burns's view of leadership had a decidedly ethical core:

> The crucial variable again is purpose. . . . I define leadership as leaders inducing followers to act for certain goals that represent the values and the motivations—the wants and needs, the aspirations and expectations—of both leaders and followers. And the genius of leadership lies in the manner in which leaders see and act on their own and their followers' values and motivations. (p. 19)

So when I asked Burns that day to define leadership for me and to tell me how one would go about recognizing a leader, his straightforward answer didn't really surprise me. He thought for a moment, and then he said, "Leadership is first and foremost a moral act. Above all, leaders must be virtuous." Although it had been more than twenty years since Burns had written his landmark book on leadership, his ideas about leadership remained essentially unchanged. In a fundamental sense, Burns has blazed the trail for all those who have come along in the past fifteen or twenty years and defined leadership in terms such as *moral, servant, transformational,* and even *soulful.* My experience with schools and school leaders over the past thirty years leads me to endorse the concepts of leadership as described by writers and thinkers such as Burns (1978), Sergiovanni (1992), and De Pree (1989), and the experiences of leaders such as Tobin, Forman, and Cervantes McGuire. Leadership is so much more than a title or a formal mandate to take charge in a particular situation. It is more than a discrete set of personal qualities or traits or the ability to perform a set of complex tasks. Leadership at its best involves more than the will of a single person to direct a group in a specific direction. The essence of leadership is a directed group will bound together by common needs, goals, beliefs, and values. To me, leadership is the ability to help create a shared vision; it is the ability both to see and to help others see beyond the present realities and glimpse the unlimited possibilities that exist in the future.

More than anything else, I believe that leaders make all the others around them want to be better both in terms of what they do and who they are as human beings. I believe that this ability is the greatest attribute any leader could ever possess. It is the ultimate compliment to any leader when he or she is able to inspire others in the organization to want to be better.

What do you believe to be the essential characteristics of effective leadership? Do you know real leadership when you see it? If so, do you know what to call it? Do you have a pretty good idea about the values, beliefs, and dreams of those who work with you in your organization? Do you make it a point to share your own values, beliefs, and dreams with your colleagues on a regular basis? Do you have a genuine appreciation for the great debt that you owe to those who trust you enough to allow you to lead? Do you derive a sense of satisfaction and even a measure of joy from the privilege of serving others in a leadership role? Do you accept the responsibility to help people become the very best that they can be? Are you truly in love with the things you do as a leader? Are you constantly looking to your right and to your left and checking your rearview mirror to be sure that you are still in the middle of the values, beliefs, and dreams of those who have trusted you to lead? The carefully chosen questions in the ensuing chapters will provide you with ample opportunities to test yourself against all these standards.

Take Time to Reflect

Take a few moments to think about some of the outstanding leaders you have been exposed to in your life. Whom do you regard as the most outstanding leader you have ever been privileged to work with? What was it that set this person apart? What qualities or characteristics made him or her such a special leader?

_____

_____

_____

_____

_____

_____

_____

_____

_____

_____

_____

_____

_____

_____

_____

_____

_____

_____

_____

What Do I Care About?

Although there are any number of important questions that leaders should ask themselves on a regular basis, I believe that none is so vital to success in a leadership role as "What do I care about?"

Why is this question so critical? It is critical because what you care about defines to a large extent who you are as a human being and as a leader. What you truly care about will dictate the things you will be passionate about, the things you will fight for, sacrifice for, and in extreme cases, even die for. Caring is the central quality that gives human beings a purpose in life—a reason to get up in the morning—even the will to live! I agree with Charles Handy (1989), who makes the point that, "Care is not a word to be found in many organizational textbooks, or in books on learning theory, but it should be" (p. 232).

I am thoroughly convinced that the things in life that you really care about and the ways in which you express the depths of that caring in your daily interactions with others are the chief determinants of whether or not your fellow human beings will trust you enough to allow you to lead.

We are all well acquainted with people in our lives who profess not to care very much about anything, and others who care deeply but whose caring is focused on the wrong things. Both the words and the actions of people who don't care and those who care about the wrong things give them away. In daily conversations, people who don't care about anything routinely send signals confirming their lack of caring. For example, you might ask them a question such as "Who do you want to win the election?" Their response goes something like this: "It doesn't make any difference, they're all a bunch of crooks anyway." Or you may ask them, "What do you want to see at the movies?" Their response: "It doesn't matter to me; none of them are any good anymore." Or you're fixing a sandwich for yourself and your uninspired friend, and you ask, "What would you like on your hamburger?" The noncaring people I am referring to frequently answer with a sad note of resignation in their voices, "I don't really care—just give me the same stuff on mine that you're having on yours."

Don't these people drive you crazy? Aren't they boring? Wouldn't you like to tell them off? Don't you think it might be a lot of fun to say, "Well I'm having Hershey's chocolate syrup on mine, and I'm more than happy to share with you!" The problem is that most of them would probably be just as happy with the chocolate syrup as not. The point is that people who don't care can never be leaders. They have no passion; they have no commitment; they have no capacity to inspire others.

A person can give away to others only the things that he or she possesses, and we all expect and deserve to receive a great deal from our leaders in terms of passion, inspiration, and commitment.

Lest we forget, there are plenty of people who care, but who care for the wrong things. In the popular motion picture *Jerry Maguire* (Brooks & Scott, 1996), the signature line that jumps out at the audience is, "Just show me the money, Jerry!" This is the admonition that the professional football star shouts to his agent, Jerry Maguire, to let him know up front that nothing else matters to him except the big payoff.

The movie portrays sports agents (even the hero, Jerry Maguire, before he comes to his senses) as ruthless killer sharks who will do anything to land clients and score a healthy percentage from their clients' lucrative contracts.

Key virtues such as love, loyalty, honor, commitment, friendship, devotion, responsibility, and integrity all take a backseat to cold, hard cash in the high-stakes, highly competitive world surrounding the marketing of professional athletes. The primary message of the movie is that unless we are careful, we can find ourselves living in a cynical world where success is measured in dollars and cents and virtues are for losers.

Most of us would agree that it would be terrible if personal greed and self-centeredness were the primary motivators for the majority of the people in the world. What would the world be like if nothing mattered except the size of a person's bank account? I don't know about you, but personally I find it reassuring to know that many, if not most of us, value a lot of things above money and the outward trappings that come with financial success. If financial success were all that really mattered in our society, then we wouldn't have so many incredibly talented and capable people devoting their lives to the education profession.

The two things that I have been discussing, a lack of caring and caring about the wrong things, can lead to cynicism in people and in organizations when carried to the extreme. Cynicism is a deadly poison; if left unfettered, it can spread from one person to another like wildfire and geometrically diminish the positive potential to accomplish the most essential and worthwhile goals in any organization.

I for one don't want to spend my work life surrounded by cynics. They drain my energy. They drag me down and suck all the joy out of living. I had an acquaintance (cynics can never be real friends to anyone, including themselves) when I was in college who we all laughingly referred to as the "black cloud." He was certain that behind every silver lining, there must be a black cloud. But just ask him to do something about it, to take an active role in solving a problem, to be personally involved and accountable for making a situation better, and watch him run away as fast as he could. He cared just enough to criticize, but never enough to make things better. Wherever he went, it was his mission in life to drag everyone else down to the depths where he resided. From his perspective, nothing was ever as it should be, and nothing ever suited him. I believe his two favorite colors must have been black and dark black. When he dies, his epitaph should read, "I told you I was sick!"

People like the "black cloud" are sad commentaries on the human condition. They stumble and bumble their way through life, criticizing without caring—expertly pointing out life's problems while deftly avoiding their responsibility to be a part of the solutions. Sadly, it almost seems as if it is mandated by law that every organization must have a few black clouds with whom to contend. I can't even imagine what daily life in an organization would be like without them, but I would surely like to know.

At the opposite extreme from those who don't care about anything or those who care only about the wrong things are the people who care a great deal about the right things. We choose these people as our leaders because they reflect our deepest-held values and convictions. They represent all the things that are good and noble in life. Despite the messiness and uncertainties of life, these people have a genuine zest for living it. They want to be involved in everything and to experience the defeats as well as the victories. Perhaps more than anything, they want to be insiders rather than outsiders in life: to be active players in the game, to have their lives count for something, and to make a real difference. I love these people! They are precisely the kind of people I want to have in my own life, because I feel and cherish their caring. You can hear their caring echoing in the passion of their voices; you can see it reflected in the glint in their eyes. It's both confirming and humanizing for me to be able to identify with the peaks and valleys of their successes and their disappointments, their victories and defeats.

Through their deep sense of caring and their caring about important things outside themselves, they make me feel alive and vital; they help me appreciate what it's like to be an insider riding the crests of the ebbs and flows of life. They make me feel as if I matter and that my own caring can make a significant difference in both my life and the lives of others. Perhaps most important, people who care make me want to be a better person than I might otherwise be without their connections to my life. Caring people are the kind of people I trust to lead me.

One night, I was sitting in my favorite chair channel surfing, when I clicked to a station where a woman was conducting an interview with the principal of an inner-city elementary school. Apparently, this principal's school was being recognized for its success in promoting high achievement for students who came from low-income backgrounds. Naturally, the program focused on the characteristics that made this school special—the things that this particular school was doing with and for children that allowed them to be successful despite their difficult economic circumstances.

During the interview, the principal recounted his first year in the school and the difficulties he had experienced coming into and adjusting to the situation. He talked about his first semester in the school and that much-needed first Christmas vacation. He talked about the first day back at school when the students returned from the Christmas break, and a conversation he had had with a second-grade student. As the principal was making the rounds of the campus, he met the student coming down the hall. The principal greeted the small boy and asked him, "Well Billy, tell me, what did you get for Christmas?" The boy's response was, "Mr. Principal, I didn't get anything for Christmas."

As the principal related this story, he became very emotional. Tears welled up in his eyes and I believe that I even saw a tear trickle down his cheek. It was both touching and inspiring for me to see this big, strong, important man moved to tears by the distressing circumstances of a single small child in his school. As he wiped the tear from his cheek, he told the interviewer, "At that precise moment, I made a vow to myself that no child in that school would ever again be able to say,

'Mr. Principal, I didn't get anything for Christmas.'" He then went on to describe how he had organized the businesses in the local community to establish a fund to ensure that every child in his school would have a happy Christmas from that day forward.

I can't tell you precisely what this particular school did to help its low-income students become academically successful, but I can venture a reasonable guess as to the reason. The school was successful because the school leader cared about the children a great deal, and although I didn't see any of the teachers interviewed, I can assure you that they cared a great deal about the children as well. I watched the remainder of the interview with keen interest. Here was a guy who was living my deepest beliefs. He summed up his leadership philosophy in a way that reflected his total commitment to helping each individual child. He said that good leaders must understand the law and bureaucracy and the policies that are a direct result of law and bureaucracy. He then added that, "If necessary, the good leader will then discard them [law, bureaucracy, and policy] and do what's best for the children."

What parent wouldn't want this man to be the principal of his or her child's school? What teacher wouldn't want to work with a principal who cared so much and demonstrated that caring in such a powerful and compelling way?

I am convinced that if everyone in the school, working together as a cohesive unit, cares enough about the children, then together they will find out what needs to be done to make the children successful and they will do everything in their power to see that it gets done! How can we ever expect parents to trust and support schools with their most precious possessions, their children, unless we who work in those schools can demonstrate beyond all doubt that we genuinely and deeply care about what happens to those children? In other words, both parents and children need to be sure that those of us in schools care a lot about the right things. This is the only way we can gain the trust and support required to be able to lead successfully.

During my time as a school principal, I sat with many parents whose children were experiencing difficulties in school. More than anything else that I could possibly have done for these parents, they wanted and deserved to see some small sign from me that I genuinely cared about their children. In all the years I've worked in and around organizations, I've never been acquainted with a successful leader who didn't care a lot about doing more for others. And I've never known a successful leader who didn't value key virtues such as love, loyalty, honor, commitment, friendship, devotion, responsibility, and integrity above personal gain. The very best leaders I've ever been associated with not only cared, they expressed their caring freely and openly on a daily basis, in ways both large and small. Maybe Autry (1991) puts it best when he says, "Good management is largely a matter of love. Or if you're uncomfortable with that word, call it caring, because proper management involves caring for people, not manipulating them" (p. 13).

Organizations cannot survive and prosper with too many people who don't care or who care only about the wrong things. Leaders must examine their values by constantly asking themselves the question, "What do I care about?" They must then light the way for others by helping to identify the key values to be embraced by the organization, and demonstrate through their thoughts and deeds that they care deeply about these values. If you care about the right things and demonstrate that caring to those around you, then they will trust you enough to grant you the permission that you need to lead.

This is not easy work! According to Beck (1994), caring involves being open to the perspectives of others, responding appropriately to the awareness that comes from that openness, and remaining committed to others in terms of the relationships that exist. Beck describes a *caring ethic* that school leaders should practice:

> First, a caring ethic would prompt leaders to assert that professional educators should take the lead in defining

values and in ensuring that schools support and nurture the development of all persons. Second, it would encourage the development of nonbureaucratic decision-making school structures. Third, this ethic would emphasize skills and competencies rather than assigned titles as determinants of organizational roles, and it would encourage the separation of role and status. Fourth, caring would prompt leaders to support collaborative efforts among and between students, teachers, and administrators. Finally, this ethic would call for structures conducive to honest, ongoing communication between persons within schools and between educators and those in the larger community. (p. 83)

In my own life, I believe that I am a person who cares a great deal. I care about things both great and small. I care about whales; I care about butterflies. I am genuinely concerned about the depletion of the ozone layer, the destruction of the Amazon rain forests, and whether or not the young people who are just starting out in their working lives will be able to support the huge numbers of baby boomers who will be retiring in the near future. I worry constantly about whether or not my own children will grow into responsible adults who are capable of taking care of themselves while caring for others as well. I also worry that I may not be able to swerve fast enough to avoid squashing that careless squirrel up the street that occasionally darts in front of my car.

Caring is the one quality in my life that gives it meaning. Two of my most important goals in life are to care more with each successive day that I live and to focus that care in the areas that matter the most.

What do you care about? Do you ever take time to reflect on the most important things in your daily life? Do you ever ask yourself, "What do I care about?" How do you demonstrate your caring to others who are central in your life? Do the structures in your school or organization support a caring ethic? What can you do to help cause your life and work environment to better reflect the things you really care about?

Take Time to Reflect

Suppose you had to suddenly give up everything you care about in your life—all your relationships with others, all your possessions, all your values—one thing at a time. What would you choose to cling to until the very end? List those things that you value the most in the space provided below, and remember to cherish them and honor them in the way you live your daily life, because they are the things that you really care about!

_____

_____

_____

_____

_____

_____

_____

_____

_____

_____

_____

_____

_____

_____

_____

_____

_____

_____

_____

What Do I Believe About People?

I think that all true leadership is indeed spiritual leadership, even if you hardly ever hear it put that flatly. The reason is that beyond everything else that can be said about it, leadership is concerned with bringing out the best in people. As such, one's best is tied intimately to one's deepest sense of oneself, to one's spirit. My leadership efforts must touch that in myself and in others.

—Vaill (1989, p. 224)

Just what do you believe about people? What kinds of things do you say to them? What do you say about them? Do you see them as being essentially good and kind and caring in their dealings with others or as evil, mean, and nasty? Do you regard most people as being lazy or industrious? Selfish or giving? Boring or interesting? Dull or ingenious? When you meet someone for the first time, do you size that person up based on the upside of his or her potential or the downside? In short, are you an optimist or a pessimist when it comes to evaluating the basic worth of your fellow human beings? The answers to these questions are critical because they define your personal personnel philosophy and determine the parameters of how you will approach others in a leadership role, as well as how others will be inclined to respond to your attempts to lead.

A few years ago, one of my colleagues offered me the opportunity to go to a medium-security prison and conduct some sessions on personal awareness with the inmates. At first, I wasn't all that excited about the opportunity. This was a totally voluntary activity for both me and the prisoners. I would be expected to go into the prison and give my time and energy to a group of men who had done some pretty awful things or they wouldn't have landed in prison in the first place.

Going in, I felt I had little in common with the prisoners. My instincts told me that if I were the least bit intelligent, I would avoid putting myself in such an uncomfortable situation. I was afraid that because I came from a world that was foreign to the one in which they lived, I wouldn't be able to relate to the prisoners at all, or I would be intimidated by them, or they might reject me and my ideas and leave me feeling totally foolish and inadequate.

Acting against my instincts, I accepted the challenge to go and work with the prisoners; to my surprise and relief, none of the unpleasant things occurred that I had imagined. The prisoners came into the meeting room at the appointed time. They took their seats in a large circle and listened intently as I explained my goals for the activities I had planned for the session that afternoon. When I talked, they were attentive; when I asked questions, they gave thoughtful responses; when I asked them to engage in a series of activities, they willingly participated. As they interacted with each other, they were unusually polite and respectful of the attitudes and opinions of others. To say that I was surprised by their behavior would be a gross understatement. I was astounded!

When I had finished my planned activities with the prisoners, they invited me to take part in a little reception they had arranged, complete with punch and cookies. As we milled about the meeting room enjoying our punch and cookies and chatting about one thing and another, I felt as if I had suddenly been transported to the *Twilight Zone*. Just a few short hours before, I could not have imagined myself sharing punch and cookies and conversation with a room full of convicted felons. As we talked together, I learned that the men who were pleasantly mingling all around me were incarcerated for a variety of serious crimes. Some of them were serving life sentences for murder, whereas others were doing time for rape or armed robbery or some other heinous misdeed. What was incredible to me when I reflected on the experience later was that if I had not had knowledge of who these men were and why they were there, I would never have known that they were capable of doing the terrible things that they had done. It almost scares me to admit it, but in many important ways, these men were exactly like you and like me.

Clearly, I had grossly underestimated the prisoners' potential as human beings and relied instead on the stereotypes that I held about criminals to shape my attitudes prior to my up-close and personal experience with them. Regardless of what else they were, they were first and foremost human beings, and I was forced to realize that given a different set of circumstances, perhaps they might have been in my place and I might have been in theirs.

This is my long-winded way of saying that we all have the potential to be a lot of things in life. In a way, the line between self-belief and self-doubt creates a prison. Although it would be pushing a point for me to say that we are all capable of turning our fellow human beings into something that they may not otherwise have become, through our faith in them and the ways we communicate that faith to them, I do believe that leaders have a responsibility to see the potential in others and to help them to realize that potential. Parker Palmer (1998) describes what that can mean for school leaders:

> Leadership in the academy means looking behind the masks we wear and perceiving our true condition. It means seeing more in teachers than teachers sometimes see in themselves—just as good teachers see more in students than students know they have. (pp. 158-159)

In my view, it is critical for leaders to believe there is a world of good to be found in every one of their fellow human beings. A leader's beliefs will shape the way in which he or she will interact with others and, in the end, impose limits or grant freedom for others to explore the potential of their humanity in an organizational setting and become the best that they can be.

In my own life, I try to shape my interactions with others through a set of beliefs that mirror my faith in the fundamental decency and goodness of people. These beliefs, which I refer to as my personal personnel philosophy, are quite simple.

First, I believe that most people are basically good and kind and caring. I believe that people are industrious, giving, interesting, and ingenious. I am quite sure that almost every person I have ever known is capable of the very best or the very worst of humankind and that it is my responsibility as a leader to find ways to free them to discover the best person that they can be in an organizational setting. De Pree (1989) reminds leaders that "People need to be liberated, to be involved, to be accountable, and to reach for their potential" (p. 97).

I believe that it is not just the individual alone, making decisions and acting on those decisions, who determines what he or she can or will accomplish in an organization but also the attitudes of others and the resulting circumstances that are an outgrowth of those attitudes. Therefore as a leader, I feel that I have a responsibility to reflect the kind of positive attitudes and caring toward my colleagues that will help shape the circumstances that promote personal growth and satisfaction for all of us working and living together in the organization.

Perhaps the most important component of my personal personnel philosophy is the belief that every individual in an organization wants to do a good job. In all my years of working in and around schools, I've never had anyone tell me or otherwise indicate by act or deed that he or she wanted to perform poorly in his or her job. When I tell some people this, they laugh at me and tell me I must be a complete fool, because they know a lot of people who clearly don't want to do a good job. To this I reply, "I would much rather be a fool than a cynic!" Cynics are deadly in an organizational setting; they have abandoned all hope and can never expect things to be appreciably better than they are or used to be.

The simple truth is that when you are seeking to discover the nature of human beings, most times you will find what you are looking to find. That's why it's essential for me to believe that everyone wants to do a good job. For if you believe that most people are lazy and don't care enough to expend the time and energy required for them to perform at a reasonably high level, then you will find ample evidence to support this conclusion. Everywhere you look in your organization, you will find lazy, careless, incompetent people trying to beat the system, intent on giving as little as possible while taking away as much as they can from the organization.

On the other hand, if you believe that everyone wants to do a good job and that each person will rise to the challenge and exert as much time and energy as is required to get the job done in a professional and caring manner, you will find just as much evidence to support this conclusion.

This is not to say that everyone in an organization is doing a good job. To believe that would indeed be foolish. There are any number of individuals in most organizations who, for one reason or another, may not be doing a good job. They may not have the skills they need to be able to perform key tasks, or perhaps they do not have the requisite knowledge central to performing their jobs well. For example, a teacher who does not have the skills needed to plan well for instruction or who is teaching out of field will have great difficulty delivering effective lessons in the classroom.

In other circumstances, people may not be sufficiently motivated to perform well, or the work setting may not be organized in such a way that they can be successful in their efforts to perform at a high level. In certain instances, we may be asking someone to do the impossible by placing them in work situations where even the best professionals might not be able to succeed (e.g., giving a beginning teacher a class of thirty-five remedial reading students without ample materials or support).

The point is that there are many reasons outside an individual's desire to do a good job that may negatively affect one's job performance. This leads to the next tenet of my personal personnel philosophy: Everyone can do a good job given the proper support and assistance.

One spring while I was an undergraduate student, I took a civil service examination and qualified for a summer job at the post office. I was excited about the opportunity because I had never held a job that paid above the minimum wage. The only drawback was that the job was in a neighboring city about thirty-five miles from where I was living at the time. The distance wasn't so much of a problem as was my unfamiliarity with the city where I would be working. People who know me well will tell you that I have a terrible sense of direction. A number of my friends go so far as to claim that I am "directionally disabled." Knowing this, my chief concern with my new job was whether I would be able to find my way around well enough in a strange city to perform the job satisfactorily. After all, I really wanted to do a good job.

When I arrived at the post office that first day to begin my job, my supervisor, a grizzled, veteran postal worker, showed me the ropes. He showed me where to get the mail that I would be delivering on my semirural route. He showed me how to sequence the individual pieces of mail to correspond with the route I would be following during delivery, and then he took me with him in the mail truck while he drove the route and delivered the day's mail. Thinking back on the experience, I remember it as a blur. Every aspect of the job, the rules, the regulations, the procedures—it was all new to me. I remember being dazed by information overload. And, to make matters worse, I was directionally disabled!

When I showed up for work the next day, my anxiety level was at a near-record high. On that second day, there was no grizzled veteran ready to take me through my paces; it was my responsibility, and my responsibility alone, to get the job done. I went to the window where I had been shown to pick up the mail for my route, received it from the clerk, and carefully began sorting it by the street addresses that were about as familiar to me as downtown Cairo, Egypt. It took me what seemed like forty forevers just to sequence the mail for delivery. By the time I had finished this preliminary chore, the other postal workers had long since departed to begin delivering their mail. At long last, I finished the mail sorting and climbed into my assigned vehicle to make my deliveries.

The first few streets on my route were close to the post office and easy enough for me to remember. I delivered a tray or two of mail at a couple of small businesses and emptied two red and blue mail drops into large, white, canvas sacks to take back to the post office with me later that afternoon. I did one or two more streets; then the world closed in on me! I was lost. I couldn't remember where to go next. The city map unfolded on the truck seat next to me didn't seem to correspond at all to the patchwork of blacktop two-lane highways and dirt roads that I was wandering over aimlessly in my big white government vehicle.

The upshot of all this is that not much mail got delivered on my route that day. Most of the people on my route must have thought it was a government holiday when they checked their mailboxes that afternoon. Thank goodness I was finally able to find the post office and park my truck. It was well after dark, and I had spent almost ten hours trying hard but failing to do what was designed as a six-hour job. I am not exaggerating when I tell you that I brought back more mail to the post office that day than I had delivered. I had the mail I had retrieved from the drop boxes and about two-thirds of the mail I had set out to deliver that morning! I felt like a miserable failure! I *was* a miserable failure!

I slunk into the post office and found the veteran who had attempted to train me the day before. He was busy at some routine task. I walked straight up to where he was working and told him point blank, "I quit!" He looked up at me from his work, and I'll never forget his cryptic response: "Nobody quits a government job!"

It took more than a little reassurance from him before I retracted my resignation and agreed to try again. The next morning, my supervisor again took me through the paces. This time, however, he did it in a more caring and considerate way. He asked me questions to make sure I understood what he was telling me, and he made me ask him questions to show that I was understanding his instructions. When we went out in the truck to deliver the mail on the route that day, he didn't assume that I knew my way around the area; he pointed out landmarks and made me write key directions on a yellow legal pad.

When we left the post office to begin the route, he brought along several indelible magic markers to write street numbers and names on quite a few of the mailboxes along the route that had previously had no markings whatsoever.

It took considerably longer than the six hours the route was supposed to require, but eventually we made it around the entire circuit. To my surprise, when we were done that evening, I had a pretty good picture in my head and on my yellow legal pad of the job that I was supposed to do.

The next day, I again had to do the route by myself. This time, however, my supervisor stopped by where I was sorting the mail to check on me, to reassure me, and to answer any last-minute questions that I might have. He also gave me a phone number and told me to give him a call if I got into trouble on the route. When I left the post office that day to begin my route, I felt entirely differently than I had two days prior. I felt I had enough information to do what I needed to do reasonably well, and I knew that in a pinch, I could call on my supervisor for support and assistance. It took me about two hours more than the six allowed to deliver the mail that day, but I got the job done.

When I returned to the post office, I walked in with my head held high. I felt like a success! I *was* a success! Within a few short weeks, I could easily perform my job in the six hours allowed. In fact, I became so proficient that I could do the job in four hours, and sometimes less. When I began returning to the post office well before I was scheduled to return, some of my fellow postal workers politely reminded me that my route was a "six-hour route" and should require a full six hours. As I recall, the way they put it was, "Hey college boy—that's a six-hour route you're running. We're still going to be delivering the mail on that route long after you've gone back to school. Don't you dare come back to this post office in less than six hours!" I got the message! From that point until the end of the summer when my job ended, I would go out on my route, finish most of my work for the six-hour day in about three hours, and then take a leisurely two-hour lunch while reading the current issues of many of my favorite magazines that I would then subsequently deliver later in the afternoon to the subscribers on my route. I can't describe how good it felt for me to be able to perform my job well, when I had come so close to walking away from it in total disgrace.

I've often wondered what would have happened if my supervisor had let me quit my job at the post office that summer so many years ago. What if he had not had enough confidence in me to encourage me to try again? I would have walked out the door feeling like a failure after my second day on the job. What if he had not taken his job as a supervisor seriously? What if he had not assumed his responsibility to help me succeed? I would have been a failure!

But he did take his responsibility as a supervisor seriously, and he did see the potential in me to get the job done. The result of this was that the job got done, and if I do say so myself, it got done in an exemplary manner. More important, I felt humanized and confident that I could succeed in other situations that would challenge my resourcefulness and resilience.

Perhaps most significant, I realized my sacred responsibility as a leader always to look for the best in others, to be sensitive to their needs in the workplace, and to do everything in my power to help them realize their potential as responsible employees and caring human beings.

This brings me to the final tenet of my personal personnel philosophy: It is the organization's responsibility and that of the leader acting on behalf of the organization to provide the necessary support and assistance required for every single person in the organization to be successful.

I am convinced that our basic beliefs about people define the limits of their potential in the workplace. Our positive beliefs about the essential goodness of people give those whom we lead the freedom to do great things; our negative beliefs predispose them to do awful things. Our basic beliefs about people encourage them to succeed on a grand scale or discourage them so that they fail miserably. Our beliefs about people give them license to become the best or the worst that they are capable of becoming. What do you believe about people? How do you communicate those beliefs in an organizational setting? How many people in your organization are struggling every day as they try vainly to meet the expectations attached to their work? What are you doing to help them in their attempts to do a good job? What are you willing to do?

> In addition to all the ratios and goals and parameters and bottom lines, it is fundamental that leaders endorse a concept of persons. This begins with an understanding of the diversity of people's gifts and talents and skills. (De Pree, 1989, p. 9)

Take Time to Reflect

So what do you believe about people? What are the basic tenets of your "personal personnel philosophy"? Take a few moments to briefly outline them in the space provided below.

_____

_____

_____

_____

Am I Willing to Share Power?

Have you ever felt that decision making in your school or organization was a game? If you felt that decision making was a game, were you also pretty sure that the winners and losers in the game were predetermined? Which side of the game were you on, and how did it make you feel? As a leader, do you trust others enough to let them in the game? Should the making of important decisions even be treated like a game? How can caring be demonstrated by leaders through the way in which decisions are made?

When I first became the principal of a high school, more than twenty years ago, I was shocked when I discovered that the people in the school didn't seem to care as much as I did. Please bear with me on this for the present—this startling declaration doesn't mean exactly what you might think it does. When I say that others in the school didn't seem to care as much as I did, I'm not being totally fair, because the standards I was using to judge caring were much different from those of the best professionals practicing in schools at that time. I was gauging caring in a rather superficial way: I equated caring in terms of the staff's willingness to perform additional tasks outside normal work responsibilities, such as sponsoring activities for students, serving on committees, and performing standing duties. For some reason or reasons unknown to me, the staff members in my school were not eager to assume these added responsibilities, and they let me know this in no uncertain terms when I made requests for their services in these areas.

At the time, it never occurred to me that some of them were already loaded down with heavy teaching responsibilities or family obligations or both. I suppose I didn't really believe that teachers should have lives outside of school. Furthermore, it never crossed my mind that most of the real professional teachers felt that there were better ways to use their time than taking tickets at football games or standing guard in the restrooms during class changes.

Whatever the reasons for rebuffing my invitations to serve, my perceptions about my colleagues' low level of caring frightened and bewildered me for two reasons. In the first place, this attitude was totally unexpected on my part. When I agreed to accept the challenge of serving as the principal of the school, I thought that everyone in the school would be as committed as I thought I was to doing everything in their power to serve and support the students, the school, and the community. I suppose this means that I thought the teachers would do exactly what I asked them to do and, furthermore, that they would be pleased as punch for the opportunities that I provided them to show me just how much they cared. I was naive enough to believe that because I was the principal, wherever I looked I would find lots of willing hands and hearts to help me with what I knew would be a formidable task. When the teachers didn't react the way I expected them to react, I was surprised and even a little shell-shocked.

The second reason I was bewildered and frightened was that I wondered how the school could ever be successful without the combined talents and commitment of all of us in the school working together to create a common vision. I thought all the teachers should get behind me and support my vision for what I believed our school could be. After all, I reasoned, I was the duly appointed leader, and a leader was supposed to have a vision. Although I hate to admit it, I was afraid that without a high level of commitment on the part of my staff to my vision for the school, the school might not live up to its promise and I might fail as a leader.

When I think back on it now, what's incredible to me is that I didn't do enough to make it appealing or inviting or even possible for my colleagues to demonstrate how much they cared. As I reflect on it, my approach was traditional; I tried to lead the school in the ways that I had seen other principals lead. I held the reins of power tightly and sought out others in the school who were comfortable with my approach and thereby appeared to me to care as much as I did. I found these highly committed individuals and made them my comrades. I gave them more than their fair share of the work and responsibility, but I also gave them more than their fair share of the attention and praise. To be frank, I played head games with the teachers to get things done the way I wanted them done, until one day the teachers decided that they had had enough of the head games, and that was the day that I got caught in my own trap.

The school where I was principal was located in a white, middle-class suburban neighborhood on the outskirts of a fairly large metropolitan area. Almost all the African American students in the school were bused from inner-city neighborhoods located about twelve miles away. Because they lived so far from the school and did not have their own transportation, most of the African American students were not involved in school life outside of taking classes. They rode their buses to school in the mornings, attended their classes, and got on their buses and returned to their neighborhoods at the end of the school day. Clearly, this was not a healthy situation for the school or the students, and I decided that we needed to do something to increase the level of involvement for our black students.

The solution proposed to address the situation was a change in the master schedule that would permit an activities period to be held during the regular school day. By reducing the time allotted to each class on a designated "Activities Friday," enough time could be gleaned to allow clubs and interest groups to meet and conduct their business. The arrangement made it possible for all students to be involved in at least one school activity even if they lived a long way from the school or had other commitments, such as after-school jobs.

It was decided that teachers who did not wish to sponsor an activity for students and students who did not choose to be involved in an activity would be paired during the scheduled activities period in a study hall arrangement.

The rest of the teachers and students would meet as scheduled and engage in their selected activities. I don't recall just how these initial decisions were made. I do recall that it was the student government association that first voiced a concern about the lack of student involvement in school activities and asked that something be done to address the situation. Beyond that, I don't recall how we made the decisions to structure the program. But regardless of how the decisions were made, we moved to the implementation stage.

The sign-up period was held, and a surprisingly large number of students and teachers opted for the study halls rather than the activities. Undaunted, we forged ahead and scheduled the first Activities Friday of the school year.

The big day came—the bell rang—the first activities period commenced—the disaster ensued! While all the teachers and most of the students went to their activities or study halls as scheduled, many did not. Students were everywhere! They were in the parking lot and out behind the gymnasium. Some even took the liberty of driving their cars to a nearby mall to purchase a hamburger and fries. Being a certifiable control freak, I was more than a little alarmed imagining all the terrible things that might happen to the students while they were supposedly under the school's supervision.

Finally, the activities period ended. We resumed our regular schedule while we counted our losses. Although no one was dead or injured, clearly the experiment had not gone well. We met with the administrative team and decided that the primary problem was not the activities period per se, but the novelty of the arrangement. After considerable discussion, we decided that both teachers and students needed more time to adjust to the innovation; we thought that one time was not enough to make a judgment about whether or not the activities schedule was a good idea. So, we went through the whole arrangement again in great detail with both students and teachers. We made sure this time that every student and teacher knew exactly where they were supposed to be and just what they should be doing during the activities period. Then we scheduled our second activities period of the year.

If the first activities period was like World War I, then the sequel could be equated with World War II! The second time we held the activities period, a lot of the students who had been in their assigned places the first time joined their fellow classmates who had opted for the parking lot, the area behind the gymnasium, and the hamburger joints. It had not seemed possible, but if anything, the second attempt was more chaotic than the first.

We were discouraged by this unexpected result, but not defeated. I called the management team together, and we again reviewed the program in detail. I was determined that we would discover what had gone wrong and devise creative solutions to the problems we were experiencing. Finally, after a lengthy discussion, we developed three alternative approaches that we thought had a reasonable chance to succeed. For the sake of simplicity, I will call the three approaches Plan A, Plan B, and Plan C. I told the administrative team that we would share the ideas with the teaching staff at our next faculty meeting and together we would make a decision as to which approach we would select for implementation. But even then, I knew in my heart that Plan A was the most desirable of the three alternatives, and I was reasonably sure that the teaching staff would endorse my preference. At the time, I had no idea that I was in for a few surprises.

The day of the faculty meeting arrived. Right before the meeting was to begin, I received my first surprise. My boss, the area superintendent of schools, dropped by the school unannounced as I was gathering my materials and preparing to head for the faculty meeting. He decided that he would accompany me to the meeting because he too was new in his position and the meeting would provide him with an opportunity to interact with the faculty. The main item on the agenda was the activities period, and although I expected it to generate some discussion, I thought that we would come to a decision—the right decision—in fairly short order.

The meeting began on time, and we proceeded rapidly through the agenda until we reached the item concerning the activities period. I told the group members that together we would explore three alternatives to correct the problems we were experiencing with the activities period. I also let them know that I expected that after some discussion, we would be able to reach a consensus on the best alternative, which we would then implement together. I explained that I preferred to reach consensus on this issue rather than decide by majority vote and that we would take all the time necessary to reach consensus. Then I briefed the teachers on the three plans and asked for discussion.

As the discussion proceeded, it was clear that both Plan A and Plan B had a good deal of support. In fact, it appeared that the faculty was pretty evenly divided on the two approaches. It was at this fatal juncture that I decided that it was time for me to demonstrate my leadership skills. I halted discussion for the moment and reviewed Plans A and B again.

Because Plan C had not generated any substantial support, we dropped it from further consideration. This time, as I explained the two plans, I was careful to enhance the advantages associated with Plan A while minimizing the disadvantages; of course, I did the exact reverse when I explained Plan B.

We then resumed discussion of the two plans, and to my amazement, not only had the number of supporters for Plan B increased, they appeared to be deeply entrenched in their positions. But I didn't give up! I continued to champion Plan A, and some of my supporters on the faculty did their best to help me carry the day. But it was a lost cause. Eventually, it was evident to everyone in the room that we would never reach consensus on a plan.

It was at this point that I gave in and told the faculty that it appeared that consensus was impossible, and therefore we would have to vote. So we voted, and I suppose I don't have to tell you which plan won a narrow victory.

After the meeting ended, the area superintendent walked back to my office with me. I think he was pretty amazed by what he had witnessed, but he didn't have too much to say about it. He did, however, have two questions for me. The first was, "Why did you waste all that time?" The second was, "Why didn't you just tell them what you wanted them to do?" To his two questions I had but one answer, and I suspect it sounded about as ridiculous to him at that time as it does to me now. I told him, "I believe in democratic leadership—I think that those who are most affected by decisions should have the right to help make those decisions."

Of course, I wasn't the least bit democratic. I was playing a game with the faculty, trying to manipulate them into believing that they were an integral part of the decision-making process when clearly they were not. And the teachers taught me a lesson by making me look foolish in front of my boss. They made it clear that they would not be manipulated by me. They let me know in a very powerful way that if I wanted to play games, they could play games, too. From that day forward, I knew that if I wanted to give them the opportunity to make a decision, I had better be prepared for them to make the decision that they wanted to make—not the one I expected them to make.

We implemented Plan B as the teachers had decided we should do. My last surprise was that it worked beautifully. That really shouldn't have been a surprise to me, I suppose; after all, it was the teachers' plan, and they were therefore committed to making it a success. Immediately after this experience, I made a silent vow never to try to manipulate the faculty again.

Shortly after that, we established a faculty steering committee in our school that was designed to place teachers at the heart of the decision-making process. Those of us on the administrative team listened carefully to the advice we received from the faculty steering committee!

What did I learn from this experience aside from making the decision to avoid engaging in gamesmanship in the future? I learned that it is not the leader's prerogative, or even his or her responsibility, to make all the important decisions in the school. If we are ever to see teachers and principals effectively leading together, then there must be some substantial changes made in the ways we think and feel about our personal and shared leadership responsibilities in the school.

I learned that if you are the formal leader, you have to give others in the organization a reason and the opportunity to demonstrate that they care by finding ways to involve them meaningfully in decision making. People naturally care a great deal more about the decisions they make than the decisions made for them by others.

Perhaps most important, I learned that a school isn't going anywhere that all of us—teachers, staff, students, and administrators—don't want it to go.

I am grateful for all these lessons. They have served me well over the years. So how about you? Are you willing to share power? Is caring demonstrated in the way in which decisions are made in your organization? If not, then what can you do about it? What are you willing to do about it?

Take Time to Reflect

Can you recall an incident when you doggedly held onto the notion of *the right decision?* What was the result? Do you think that there could have been a better result if you had been more open to the ideas of others in this particular situation? If you had it to do over, what would you do differently?

_____

_____

_____

_____

_____

_____

_____

_____

_____

_____

_____

_____

_____

_____

_____

_____

_____

_____

_____

_____

_____

_____

_____

Do I Care Enough to Do the Little Things?

We can do no great things, only small things with great love.

—Mother Teresa

More than twenty years ago, I received an invitation to attend the Tournament Players Golf Championship in Florida. Because I like golf and had never been to a major professional tournament before, I was excited about the opportunity. I got up before the crack of dawn that first morning of the tournament and drove to the course where it was being played. I arrived at the tournament site well before the gates were opened to spectators. That was perfectly okay with me, because I didn't want to miss a single moment.

The first players out on the course that morning were known in the golfing profession at that time as *rabbits.* I'm not sure why they were called rabbits, but it had something to do with the fact that they were not among the elite group of about 150 or so players who were exempt from qualifying for tournaments each week based on their official earnings from the tournaments they had competed in during the previous year. Because rabbits had not won enough money (some hadn't won any) to be in the exempt group, they had to compete with each other before the start of the regular tournament each week to earn a place in the tournament field. In short, rabbits had to play an unofficial tournament and do well to get into the official tournament. I suppose they were called rabbits because they hopped around the country from tournament site to tournament site each week, hoping to qualify for a chance to win money in a Professional Golfers Association tour event. (Unfortunately, most rabbits won little money, if any, and eventually they hopped their way into golf obscurity.)

I was out on the course as an observer early that first morning as the rabbits made their way around the golf course. The thing I remember most is the wonderful skills these nonexempt players, these golfing vagabonds, exhibited as they played their shots. Their drives were long and straight. Their short games were a thing of beauty as they nestled their iron shots mere feet from the pin. The touch they displayed on their putts would make a skilled surgeon turn green with envy. They were wonderful players in every respect. As I watched them display their marvelous skills, the thing that amazed me most was that these players didn't make any money playing golf! That's why they were rabbits. If they had made a reasonable amount of money from their play, they would be exempt players.

All that morning and into the afternoon, I watched the exempt players as they played their way around the course. Like the rabbits who had come through ahead of them, they too possessed extraordinary skills, which they displayed time after time with their powerful drives and precision shot making. But just by watching, I could not distinguish any real differences between the rabbits and the exempt players. I saw some of the greatest players in the world that day, including

Arnold Palmer, Jack Nicklaus, Lee Trevino, and Gary Player, but I could not distinguish what made their golf games superior to the golf games played by the rabbits.

When I thought more about it, it became evident that the difference between worldwide fame and fortune as a professional golfer and total obscurity is slight indeed. In fact, the difference is so small, it is imperceptible to the naked eye. Yet however small that difference might be, it is real—and it has proven over the years to be tremendously significant in making or breaking countless golfing careers.

Since my trip to the Tournament Players Championship those many years ago, I have come to believe that it is always the little things and not the big things that determine whether or not a person will be successful in almost any endeavor in life. The margin between success and failure is always slight, and everybody will do the big things because the big things are always required. It is the person who is willing to do the little things, those things that are not required but are voluntary, who will always gain the edge in meeting the challenges life places before us. This is true because success in any endeavor is highly discriminating and always favors those who are willing to go the extra mile—those who demonstrate an uncommonly high level of commitment by their willingness to do not just the big things but also the little things.

Consider for a moment what it means to be or to have a best friend. Do you ever think about what it means to be a best friend? The term *best friend* certainly means better than average; it even means better than good. It means best! But what is it about a best friend that makes that person the best?

A person is certainly not a best friend because he or she does or says what's expected of a friend in every situation or circumstance. A person earns the mantle of best friend because that person consistently goes beyond what is expected and frequently does the unexpected in a particular situation or circumstance.

Suppose for a moment that it is your birthday. People, including your best friend, may give you cards and even an assortment of gifts. But that's expected—after all, it is your birthday. But what about all those days when it's not your birthday? What about that one particular day when you're feeling really down and nobody seems to notice or even care—nobody, that is, except your best friend, who may send you flowers or take you out to dinner just to cheer you up. It is precisely this kind of commitment and caring about you— the willingness to go beyond what is expected—that makes your best friend so special. It is going the extra mile, doing the little things to exhibit extraordinary caring and commitment, that makes your best friend the best rather than just average or good.

In my almost thirty-five years in education, I have never known a highly successful leader, whether it be teacher or administrator, who failed to pay attention to the little things. The so-called little things have set these leaders apart from their peers.

I have yet to visit a school where the school leaders didn't have some means to organize students and teachers, a curriculum in place, textbooks and materials available, established policies and procedures for dealing with daily school life, and so forth. Those are big things, and they are required of all schools.

Just because all those things are in place, though, doesn't demonstrate that a school has reached a high level of caring for students. I've never seen a teacher who didn't open the door for his or her students to enter the classroom in the morning, who didn't try to deliver some kind of knowledge to the students in one way or another, or who failed to assign work for the students and give some kind of grade at the end of the marking period. These are not matters of choice—these are not little things, they are big things. These are fundamental things required of all teachers.

I have yet to experience a school or a classroom where the big things made a real difference in terms of the overall quality of the educational experience that children received. It's always the little things that set schools and classrooms apart and make them exceptional places for children to be. But exactly what are those little things? What makes them so special?

When I first became a high school principal, I decided that I needed to do some things to demonstrate my caring and commitment to the students, the teachers, and the community. I thought it would be a good idea to single out some of the children who were experiencing academic and behavioral problems at school and visit them in their homes. Each week, I selected a child who was having a particularly difficult time at school and dropped by his or her home in the afternoon. These visits were always unannounced. I would just drive up to the kid's house, get out of my car, go inside, and visit with whomever was available and had a vested interest in the kid's future. Sometimes I would catch a mother frying chicken in the kitchen while preparing to go to her second job later that evening. The house might be in total disarray, and someone might be passed out on the couch. In such instances, I would sit on a stool in the kitchen and talk with the mother about her child while she continued with her cooking. At other times, when I arrived at the kid's house, there might not be a father or a mother, but a grandmother who had taken on the responsibility of raising her grandchildren. If that were the case, then I would sit with that grandmother on a sofa in the living room and talk about what we could do at school to help her grandchild succeed.

No matter what the circumstances were, the trip was always worthwhile for two reasons. The first was that my willingness to go into the community and talk about the child's educational problems rather than asking the community to come to me at the school was tangible evidence that I cared about the children in my school. It was evidence that I cared even about those children who were doing poorly or who were troublesome. Most people would probably say that my job as a principal didn't require me to go to children's homes and visit with their families after work; home visits were not specifically included in my official job description. I went to visit in children's homes not because I had to, but because I wanted to demonstrate that I cared about the children. And I did care about them!

The second reason that the trips were worthwhile was that they revealed to me in bold and living color the kinds of home environments that some of our unsuccessful students were forced to deal with in their everyday lives. Sometimes I was shocked by what I experienced, but I needed to be shocked. It made me more sensitive and empathetic toward these students; it allowed me to be more patient with them as I sought solutions to their educational problems.

Given the broad range of responsibilities I had as principal of the school, my weekly visits in the community were small things. They were so small, in fact, that they weren't specifically included in my job description. Nobody ever asked me about them. Nobody even knew that I made these visits, with the exception of those kids and their families who were the recipients of my unexpected social calls. But I remain convinced that my home visits were some of the more important things that I did, because they were highly visible signs for our children and their caretakers of my commitment to children who were experiencing difficulties in our school. Successful school leaders will always find ways to show commitment and caring.

Some people I know spend hours and hours writing thank-you notes to students, teachers, and community members for contributions they have made to the school or to the children in the school. These leaders may bring flowers from home and put them in the teacher work room to brighten up the environment. They take the time to learn the name of the part-time worker in the lunch room and remember to ask how her grandchildren enjoyed their visit with her over the summer.

Successful leaders never fail to find ways to encourage others when they make mistakes and their confidence is shaken. They smile and show good humor even when things are at their worst, because they know how important it is to radiate hope in such circumstances. While walking across the campus, these special people will always stoop to pick up a piece of paper littering the grounds, to demonstrate in a small but significant way the pride and care they feel for their school and the people who inhabit that school.

A couple of years ago, one of my closest friends lost his father after an extended illness. The funeral was scheduled for the middle of the week at a site about 900 miles round-trip from where I lived at the time. At first, I thought I would purchase a really nice funeral bouquet and send it to express my family's sympathy, but not attend the funeral because of the time and the travel involved. This would have been the expected thing for me to do in this circumstance, given the great distance that would have to be traveled to attend the funeral, the fact that the funeral was being held in the middle of the work week, and how busy my work schedule was at the time. On reflection, however, I decided that I should take a few days and drive to the funeral because I knew it would mean a great deal to my friend. Had he known of my plans to attend, he would have tried to discourage me from making the trip. He knew how busy I was at the time, and he's the kind of person who always puts the needs of others ahead of his own.

I arrived at the funeral chapel shortly before the appointed time. When my friend came out into the chapel and saw me there, he didn't have to say anything—I could tell from the expression on his face that he was moved by my presence there. My presence touched him because he didn't expect me to come, but I had come anyway. The fact that I had made the decision to attend the funeral wasn't a big thing by any stretch of the imagination, but it would be hard for anyone to deny that it was a significant thing, at least from the perspective of my friend.

The day after we returned home from the funeral, my friend again thanked me for taking the time and driving all that distance to show my support for him. I thought about what he was saying to me, and I realized something that I believe is important. My reply to his expression of gratitude was, "Life affords us too few opportunities to show others how much we care; we can't afford to waste those opportunities." I didn't have to say any more. My friend is a very caring person and an extraordinary leader. He understands well that the little things are, in fact, the most important things.

Each summer, the Department of Education in our university sponsors an institute for teacher leaders in Southern

California. The institute is a powerful expression of the University of La Verne's commitment to the professional development of teachers in the region. Although I think that the entire institute is a truly wonderful event, I am particularly touched by one of the activities that is always a part of the experience. On the last day of the institute, the organizers, Tom McGuire and Peggy Redman, present each participant with a beautiful crystal apple. Although the apples are given to the participants, participants aren't permitted to keep them. Each person must in turn give the apple to a teacher from his or her past; it must be presented to a teacher whose influence was of great significance in that individual's personal and professional growth and development.

I've often wondered what it must feel like for a teacher to receive the gift of one of those apples unexpectedly. The apple is a small thing in terms of its value, but an enormous thing in terms of the effect it has on a recipient. But then, it's always the little things that are the big things!

By the way, I gave my crystal apple to my former high school math teacher, Harmon Fowler. He taught me math for the four years that I was in high school, and a class in physics as well. Although he was a far better math teacher than I was a math student, it wasn't just his knowledge of math and how to teach it that made him so special. What made Harmon so special was that he genuinely cared about every single student in his classes, and we knew it. Even after we graduated and went away in search of our dreams, he continued to follow our progress and to rejoice at our victories and to encourage us through our defeats. On Harmon's seventieth birthday, my wife, Nancy, and I (she'd had Harmon as her math teacher as well) drove over to Atlanta to attend his birthday party. Two other former students were also in attendance at the party, even though none of us had taken a class from him for more than thirty years. I gave Harmon my crystal apple on behalf of all the hundreds of students whose lives he had touched over the years. I didn't realize how much the apple meant to him at that time, but when he died last year, his wife, Anita, called to tell us about his passing and to let us know how much he had treasured his crystal apple.

Successful leaders recognize and appreciate the importance of the little things to the overall health and vitality of an organization. They realize that by going beyond broad expectations and demonstrating commitment through small but significant acts of caring, they can build an environment that will bring out the best in everyone.

How about you? Do you believe in going the extra mile? Have you demonstrated to others how much you care with countless little acts of kindness, or have you wasted those rare opportunities to show others how much you really care? What are some of the little things that you can do in your present work environment to demonstrate your caring? What are you waiting for?

Take Time to Reflect

Suppose you had the opportunity to present a beautiful crystal apple to one of your former teachers. Who would you give the apple to, and why would she or he be selected? Maybe you should just do it!

_____

_____

_____

_____

_____

_____

_____

_____

_____

What Does It Mean
to Be Responsible?

There is an old story about an aspiring young administrator who received a telephone call out of the blue from
the local school superintendent, late one afternoon in early
August. The superintendent told the young man that he had
some bad news and some good news. The bad news was that
the school board had just made a decision to fire the principal
of the local high school, who had been on the job for many
years. The good news was that the superintendent had nomi-
nated the young fellow as the replacement for the veteran
principal and the school board had unanimously endorsed his
nomination. The superintendent congratulated the new principal on his selection and advised him to get right over to the
high school and relieve his predecessor.

The young man was torn by conflicting emotions as he
drove over to the high school to carry out the directive of the
superintendent. He liked the old principal and was genuinely
sorry to see his administration end this way. On the other
hand, being appointed to the principalship of the local high
school at such a tender age was a great boost to his career as

an educational leader, and he felt both excited and exhilarated at the unexpected opportunity that had fallen into his lap. As he drove to the school, he wondered about the reception he would receive from the departing principal. Clearly, the veteran principal would not be pleased that his contract had been canceled by the board, and the young man fully expected that he would not receive a very warm welcome from the man he was succeeding.

The newly appointed principal was quite surprised when he arrived at the school and was graciously received by the old principal. The veteran seemed totally unaffected by his recent misfortune. He even appeared to be somewhat jovial in his demeanor. He smiled at his replacement's obvious discomfort and told him not to be concerned in the least. He explained that he had known that his days were numbered for some time and that he was frankly relieved that the ax had finally fallen and he could get on with his life and his career. The veteran principal smiled as he told the younger man that if he had to be replaced, he was gratified that his replacement would be someone he admired and respected. To prove his point, he told the new principal that he was going to give him something that would help him as he made the transition to the principalship.

With that, he placed two sealed envelopes, marked #1 and #2, in the new principal's hand and said, "Take these two envelopes and put them in a safe place. A time will come when you will face a difficult crisis that you won't be able to solve no matter what you try. When that time comes, take out the first envelope and read the contents. The words I have written will help you extricate yourself from the crisis that you are facing." He sternly cautioned the new principal not to use the envelopes unless he had exhausted every other possibility first. The veteran principal then warmly shook his successor's hand, handed him the keys to the building, climbed into his car, and drove away.

The new principal placed the two envelopes in his top desk drawer and soon forgot all about them. For a time, things went well for him and the school. The students, the teachers, and the community had grown tired of the old administration. They liked the new man, and everyone went out of the way to help the new principal succeed. The new principal enjoyed an extended "honeymoon" that stretched out over most of the first year. Then suddenly, without warning, it happened. A seemingly routine problem presented itself. The principal applied what he thought was the proper solution, but the problem didn't go away—instead, it grew more ominous. The principal tried another solution, but that solution produced the same result as the first solution, and the problem only increased in size and intensity. A little alarmed by this time, the principal tried a third solution and was terrified when the problem spun out of control and substantially disrupted the entire school and even spilled over into the community.

Suddenly, it seemed as if the principal's friends and supporters had become scarce. Meanwhile, his constituents grew more restless and impatient for a solution to the crisis with each passing day. The young man began to panic.

He racked his brain for a way out of the crisis. Just when all seemed lost, he remembered the envelopes that had been given to him by the man he had succeeded. He raced to his office, jerked open the top drawer of his desk, and felt for the envelopes. He found the first one, eagerly ripped it open, and read the message inside, which said, "Blame it on me!" He was dumbstruck. "Blame it on me?" he muttered.

Then he understood. He called a staff meeting and announced that the crisis the school was facing was not of his doing. He told them that the present situation was the direct result of poor decisions that had been made by his predecessor and that he, because of his lack of involvement in those poor decisions, was blameless. The people listened, and the principal was relieved as he saw some of them begin to nod their heads in agreement. Soon, they were all nodding and agreeing that the old principal was indeed the responsible party. Thanks to the sage message in that first envelope, a disaster had been averted. The young principal breathed a deep sigh of relief, thanked his lucky stars, and paid sincere tribute in his heart to his wise old predecessor.

Things in the school returned to normal. For quite a while, everything ran like clockwork, and the young principal relaxed and grew more comfortable in his leadership role. But alas! One day another crisis began to emerge. Like the first crisis, it grew and grew, no matter what course of action the principal took to resolve the situation. After much reflection and a fair amount of teeth gnashing, the principal remembered that he still had an envelope that he had not yet used. "Thank goodness!" he exclaimed as he raced to his office to retrieve his salvation from the top desk drawer. He searched frantically for the magic envelope, grasped it in his sweaty palm, and gleefully ripped it open. The simple message contained in the envelope read, "Prepare two envelopes!"

The message in this little story is unmistakable. When all is said and done, the leader is the person with the ultimate responsibility. He or she cannot pass that responsibility along to someone else in times of crisis. Some leaders can get by on their good looks, personalities, or political connections for a while. Some can get by for a time by blaming others for their own shortcomings. But at some point, a day of reckoning is bound to come, and the leader's mettle will be tested.

During my first year as a high school principal, I received a lot of lessons in responsibility. One that stands out took place during that fall. In South Carolina, school personnel were required to fill out annual basic educational data survey (BEDS) reports. These reports were designed to help the South Carolina Department of Education monitor personnel and programs throughout the state by systematically collecting information related to teachers' areas of certification and teaching assignments, as well as other information critical to providing all students with a defined minimum program. A portion of the BEDS report was especially designed to be answered by the principal of a school. This section of the report, which was referred to as "the list of assurances," presented fifty general statements related to school program standards, to which the principal was required to respond with a simple "yes" or "no," depending on whether or not the principal judged the standard to be met or not met. It was sort of an honor system of school accountability. The fifty items ran the gamut from health room facilities to playground areas to instructional leadership. In fact, the first item contained in the list of assurances pertained to the principal's responsibility to provide instructional leadership and was stated something like this: "The principal spends 50% of his or her time in instructional leadership." As it turned out, completing that list of assurances for the first time created quite a dilemma for me.

I recall sitting at my desk, sharpened No. 2 pencil in hand, ready to discharge my responsibilities by completing the principal's portion of the BEDS report. I was stumped, however, by that first item on instructional leadership. Although I was reasonably certain that the desired response to the item, "The principal spends 50% of his or her time on instructional leadership," was "yes," I was even more certain that the more truthful response was "no." Technically, the correct response wasn't even included in either of the two choices that had been provided for me. The correct response would have been something like, "You've got to be kidding!" or "You have definitely lost your mind if you think principals can spend 50% of their time in instructional leadership!"

One of the advantages of being a rookie principal in a large school district is that there is always someone older and wiser to answer questions for you. The person I chose to answer this particular question for me was the secondary supervisor in the district office. He had been a successful principal in the district for a number of years prior to earning his district office assignment, and I felt comfortable sharing my dilemma with him. So, I called him on the telephone, and the conversation went something like this:

Me: Don, I'm having a problem completing the assurances section of the BEDS report.

Don: What's your problem?

Me: I don't know how to answer the first item. It says the principal spends 50% of his or her time in instructional leadership.

Don: Mark it "yes."

Me: Don, I know I'm probably expected to mark the item yes, but the truth is, I don't spend 50% of my time in instructional leadership. I'll bet I don't even spend 10% of my time in instructional leadership.

Don: Hell! Mark it "yes"! Everybody marks it "yes"!

I politely thanked Don for his assistance, hung up the telephone, and marked the question "no." After all, I was a brand-new principal—I still had my integrity! And just to demonstrate how much integrity I had, I marked six or seven other items "no" as well. I completed my report, bundled it up with the teachers' finished reports, and sent the whole thing off to my assigned supervisor in the department of education. I thought that would be the end of it. I had done my duty while preserving my integrity. I had answered each of the items as honestly as I could, and I was feeling pretty good about myself.

Sometime around the end of November that year, I received an unexpected response to my BEDS report from my supervisor in the department of education. For each of the items to which I had responded "no," he had two more questions for me to answer. The first question was "Why not?" The second question was "What do you plan to do about it?" As an added bonus for the honesty I had displayed, I received a letter of reprimand from my district superintendent for making the district look bad!

The answer to the first question, "Why not?" was complex. There were a lot of reasons why not. I was a new principal struggling hard just to survive in an alien environment. I didn't know how to be an instructional leader. Somehow, they'd forgotten to teach me that in graduate school, and I hadn't bothered to learn how during my two years as an assistant principal in a different school in the district. To complicate matters further, the learning curve was huge for me at that time in my career, and I was spending inordinate amounts of time on routine tasks that would have been better left to others. Unfortunately, I hadn't yet learned how to delegate effectively. Even if I had known how to delegate, I didn't know the staff well enough to know who could do what best. There were a lot of other reasons I could have come up with to justify why not, but I think you get the point.

As for my supervisor's second question, "What do you plan to do about it?" that answer was much more simple than the answer to the "Why not?" question. From that day forward I planned to check "yes"!

Once I had recovered from the shock of being taken to task, I was able to think more about the two questions my supervisor had posed for me. On reflection, I was forced to admit to myself that they were reasonable questions and I was the one who had the responsibility to answer them in a satisfactory manner. If I wasn't spending 50% of my time in instructional leadership, and that was the expectation for the principal of a school, then I had damn well better find a way to do it. If my health room was inadequate or my playgrounds unsuitable, then it was my job to see that these situations were remedied. It wasn't enough for me smugly to check "no" on an annual survey from the department of education. It was my responsibility to work within the system to do whatever was required to make the answer "yes"!

So what does responsibility mean to you? Do you willingly embrace the responsibility that goes along with leadership? Are you always prepared to accept responsibility for your own actions as well as to share responsibility for the actions of those you lead? Can you resist the temptation to blame others for poor decisions? Are you willing to share the credit for your successes while shouldering the blame alone for your failures?

Take Time to Reflect

Suppose that for some reason or other, you were suddenly forced to leave your present position, and you genuinely wanted to do your successor a favor by leaving two pieces of advice in separate envelopes that would help him or her to lead successfully. What advice would you provide in each of your "two envelopes"?

(1) _____

_____

_____

_____

_____

_____

_____

_____

_____

(2) _____

_____

_____

_____

_____

_____

_____

_____

_____

Am I Willing to
Jump for the Brass Ring?

F or the last several years I was at the University of South
Carolina, I taught a leadership institute each spring with
two of my female colleagues. My colleagues had started the
institute five or six years earlier and restricted enrollment to
women because they correctly assumed that women leaders
face a number of unique obstacles that need special attention. By
designing an institute especially for women, they reasoned that
they would be able to confront these obstacles head-on without
the distraction of always having to justify their content and
methodology to a group of males who had absolutely no idea
where they were coming from. Their plan worked pretty well!
So well, in fact, that they eventually decided that it was time to
bring men into the conversation and see if men and women
could talk to each other about what it means to lead from both
the male and the female perspectives. So, the institute was
opened to men for the first time, and I was given the opportunity to team teach the institute with my two female colleagues.

The leadership institute is continually evolving, with the
frequent addition of new ideas and activities. The first couple

of years, the institute included a set of exercises known as the "ropes course." The ropes course is a set of team-building activities that drive home the importance of communication and cooperation to accomplishing group and individual goals. The first year that we used the ropes course, we included only the "low-ropes" exercises because we didn't know how many of our students would be willing to participate in the "high ropes." The low-ropes exercises, although challenging in many respects, allow participants to keep one foot on the ground at all times. The high-ropes exercises, on the other hand, take place high above the ground. Finally, we decided that we should give participants an opportunity to stretch themselves a little if they were so inclined. We added the option of participating in some exercises on the high ropes.

At this point, I should mention that I personally do not enjoy being in high places. I make it a habit always to keep at least one foot firmly planted on terra firma. In fact, I would like flying a whole lot better if airplanes taxied from one city to the next rather than becoming airborne. So, as you can probably guess, including the high-ropes exercises in the institute was not my idea!

The students in the institute had the option of participating in one of two exercises on the high ropes. One of these exercises produced some unexpected and even wonderful results. It requires the participant to climb a telephone pole by grasping small rings attached to either side of the pole. When the participant arrives near the top of the pole, which is about thirty or so feet off the ground, he or she must pull up and stand with both feet on top of the pole. If you think this sounds difficult, you should stand on the ground and look up at the top of the pole.

This exercise is not the least bit dangerous, it just feels dangerous—real dangerous! The participant is protected from falling during the exercise by a harness fastened around the waist and secured to a rope-and-pulley security system that is capably manned by a team of fellow participants on the ground.

Once a participant has successfully climbed the telephone pole and is standing with both feet firmly planted on top of the summit, the next challenge is to jump off the pole and attempt to grasp a trapeze suspended at eye level approximately six to eight feet from the pole. If the participant successfully grasps the trapeze, the exercise is completed and the triumphant (trust me, this is the right word) warrior is then lowered slowly to the ground by the pulley, to be greeted by the love and adoration of fellow participants. If the participant jumps and fails to grasp the trapeze, then, after a sudden jolt resulting from the falling human body being jerked to a halt by the rope attached to the harness, the participant is slowly lowered to the ground, to be greeted by the love and adoration of fellow participants.

The glorious reception one receives on the ground is not reserved for participants who are successful in grasping the trapeze. The reception is given to all those who successfully conquer their fears enough to climb all the way to the top of the pole and make the leap. The participants, who have already jumped themselves or are waiting to jump, understand that the real accomplishment is not in grabbing the brass ring; it is in trusting yourself and your colleagues enough to make the leap. If the truth be known, it is probably a far greater accomplishment to jump and miss the trapeze than it is to jump and grasp it successfully.

We were amazed that first time as we watched students perform on the high ropes. There were some we knew would relish the opportunity to show what they could do, and they didn't disappoint us. We were overwhelmed, however, by a number of others who surprised us by not only accepting the challenge but also conquering their fear.

The classic example was a young Korean woman who hadn't been in the country long enough to build close friendships. As she climbed the pole, she was obviously terrified. Her hands shook, and her voice faltered when she attempted to speak. When she arrived near the top of the pole, she hesitated a long time before she was finally able, with the encouragement of her fellow participants, to pull herself all the way up until she was standing with both feet on the top. Looking up from thirty feet away, we could all clearly see that fear gripped the heart of the small figure balancing precariously on the summit of the pole. Several times, she started to climb down without attempting to jump to the trapeze, but her colleagues on the ground wouldn't permit her to stop short of her goal. They assured her that she could do it and that they were there to catch her if she should miss.

After what seemed like an eternity, she gave in to the overwhelming wave of support that was radiating up from the ground. She jumped into space and missed the trapeze, only to be saved by the safety harness. A roar of approval went up from the ground below. As she was safely lowered to the ground by the rope attached to the safety harness, she received more love and adoration from the group than anyone else who attempted the exercise the entire day. I am convinced that this happened because everyone realized just how much more courage it required for her to perform the exercise than had been required from any of the others who attempted the feat that day.

Leadership feels a lot like standing on top of that pole and looking out into space. In fact, the practice of leadership is much like a series of ropes courses, all with varying degrees of difficulty. The leader is constantly confronted with a challenge. In every situation, he or she must weigh the potential to realize gain against the potential to experience loss and even, at times, total disaster. The need to feel safe is powerful, but the rewards that come with personal, professional, and organizational growth are equally alluring. Only the person standing on the top of the pole, the leader, can decide whether the anxiety produced by the fear of falling is such a powerful deterrent that it prohibits one from even trying—or if the excitement of the jump, the exhilaration of soaring like a bird through the air, is satisfying enough to encourage one to do it again and again.

Whether or not a leader chooses to jump off the top of the telephone pole is not only dependent on weighing the balance of the potential risks versus the rewards but also on the kind of organization that the leader has built around himself or herself.

Some leaders build organizations where risk is avoided at all cost. The chief goal of such organizations invariably becomes safety rather than growth. Not only does the leader avoid risks, but he or she discourages others in the organization from taking the unnecessary chances that always accompany trying new and different things. Over time, these organizations become stagnant; they lose their edge and become boring and unrewarding places to work.

Other leaders build organizations where risk taking is encouraged and effort is celebrated and rewarded just as much as success. Such leaders are never out on the high wire alone. They build a safety net of mutual trust and respect that can sustain them in case they fall. These risk-taking leaders are the best leaders because the organizations they lead are dynamic and vital: They encourage human beings to test their limits to the maximum and to taste the sweet nectar of success.

A number of years ago, I was a member of a team of researchers that conducted a national study of high school principals and their schools. One of the things that emerged from our study was a clear relationship between risk-taking behavior and school success. We discovered that when principals, teachers, and other staff members had healthy appetites for risk, they were more likely to experience positive growth. In fact, we became convinced that the more risks, the bigger the risks, and the more people involved in risk-taking behavior, the better the results.

An appetite for risk, especially in public schools, may be especially important because of the highly bureaucratic nature of schools and school systems, most of which have hierarchies of top-level managers who fear the uncertainties of dealing with the unknown and tend to be inflexible and resistant to change. It's been my unhappy experience that most school boards are even more resistant to change and the risks associated with doing things in a different way than are the school leaders they entrust with the daily management of the organization. In this kind of environment, it is no wonder that calculated risk taking can lend an air of excitement and energy to schools that helps relieve the institutional boredom that saps the vitality of principals, students, and teachers day after day, week after week, month after month, and year after year.

Why are some leaders willing to take risks while others choose always to play it safe? The best leaders take risks not because they are foolhardy or careless, but because they realize the effect that risk-taking behavior has on others. Risk-taking leaders are not "loose cannons on deck." On the contrary, they are thoughtful planners who realize that a failure today doesn't preclude success in the future but that a failure to *try* will surely preclude success in the present as well as the future.

Everyone who wishes to lead must realize that any worthwhile pursuit involves a significant element of risk. A successful business leader might take a gamble on a new product line; a world-class ice skater in the heat of competition might disdain a simpler maneuver and go for the risky triple jump, risking everything for the chance to win it all. Think about it. Did you ever see an ice skater win an Olympic gold medal by doing a simple routine perfectly? I don't believe that I ever have or that I ever will.

The most successful role models in any endeavor are those willing to risk a temporary failure for the opportunity to experience long-term success. In a spine-tingling scene from the popular movie *Top Gun* (Simpson, Bruckheimer, & Scott, 1993), the brash young aviator played by Tom Cruise flies his Tomcat jet fighter upside down mere inches from a Russian MIG. Behavior like that is a far cry from the standard operating procedures outlined for naval pilots, but it shows the mettle of those considered to be the best of the best—the so-called top guns!

Like business leaders, ice skaters, and fighter pilots, teachers and principals take risks, at least the extraordinary ones do. A teacher who is willing to look foolish by running around the classroom flapping her arms to dramatize the flight of Icarus is so much more exciting, inspiring, and wonderful than one who won't. I've witnessed one of the finest teachers in the school where I served as principal in just such a display. By the way, she was one of those very special teacher leaders who cared tremendously about the school and the students and showed that caring in countless ways. Believe me, the students loved her for her willingness to make herself vulnerable! I loved her for it too and wished that I could find a way to encourage all the teachers in our school to run around and flap their arms on a more regular basis.

Risk-taking leaders understand that taking occasional risks is part and parcel of soaring with the eagles. They also realize that by taking risks, they are making themselves vulnerable to the criticism and second-guessing of others with less stout hearts. They are, however, more than willing to subject themselves to second-guessing because they know that by making themselves vulnerable, they encourage others in their organizations to do the same. They understand that if, as principals, they take risks with and for teachers, then teachers will be much more likely to take risks with and for students. I believe that most of us would agree that the most significant growth experiences we have had in our lives required a certain measure of risk.

Are you a risk taker? When did you last take a big gamble? When was the last time you took on a job that you weren't certain you could master? Successful leaders take such risks frequently, trusting their instincts more than evidence or even experience.

What kind of school atmosphere do you prefer, one that is soothing and peaceful or one that is exciting and sometimes verging on chaotic? A risk taker will occasionally risk chaos to foster an air of excitement.

How often have you made important decisions without checking with your boss? Risk takers rush in where angels fear to tread; however, they consider the consequences as well as the rewards.

Do you seek to draw new people and groups into your projects? Do you make the initial contact, or do you wait to be contacted? Risk takers are recruiters; they roust collaborators out of the woodwork.

When one of your projects blows up in your face, do you blame someone else, laying low until the smoke clears, or do you accept full responsibility? Risk takers recognize the implications of failing and are willing to take the responsibility for failure going in and coming out. They know that it is far easier to ask for forgiveness than it is to seek permission.

It has been my experience that people who enjoy the challenges associated with risks often have great energy and active, creative minds. They are secure people who are basically happy, successful, confident, and competent. They are, above all, optimists who believe they can control their own destinies and are more than willing to take a few risks in their attempts to do so.

Unfortunately, it seems that in our schools today, risk takers are an endangered species. I've observed in hundreds of schools over the years, and I am quite convinced that true risk-taking behavior is quite rare. I suppose that in some ways, risk-taking behavior in schools is a little like an automobile accident: Sometimes you can go for months and even years and not see a single accident and then, all of a sudden, you may see several in one day. Like a car accident, risk-taking behavior can be dramatic and even traumatic. But unlike car accidents, risk-taking behavior is an extremely powerful and creative force that can breathe new life into stale, stolid, and worn-out organizations. Wheatley (1992) suggests that leaders need to be responsible inventors and discoverers. To accomplish this, however, leaders require the "courage to let go of the old world, to relinquish most of what we have cherished, to abandon our interpretations about what does and doesn't work" (p. 5). In other words, leaders need the courage to be risk takers.

Schools today are not places for the faint of heart. We don't need more school leaders in search of safety! On the contrary, we need more risk takers in boardrooms, classrooms, and principals' offices. We need more school leaders like the young Korean woman. She stood at the top of the pole that day and found the courage she needed in herself and the confidence she needed in her colleagues in order to jump for the brass ring. She is a better person today for risking so much to conquer her fear, as are all of us who witnessed her courage. Maybe that's why she received more love and adoration from the group than anyone who attempted the feat that day!

Take Time to Reflect

Think about a time in your life when you had to summon all the courage at your disposal to attempt to do something that you were really afraid to do. What did you decide to do, and what were the results? Were the rewards worth the risks? If you had it to do over again, would you make the same decision? Why or why not?

_____

_____

_____

_____

_____

_____

_____

_____

_____

_____

_____

_____

_____

Am I Taking Care of My Water Buffalo?

10

W hat gives some of us the right to lead and others the responsibility to follow? What are the costs and rewards of leadership? Of followership? What is the responsibility of leaders to demonstrate caring and compassion for those who dutifully and willingly follow their lead? How well have you taken care of those whom you have led?

One of the greatest experiences of my life was spending a year in the Philippines as a Fulbright Scholar during the late 1980s. A lot of experiences made the year remarkable. Most people would consider the great majority of those experiences to be insignificant if taken individually, but together, they added up to a life-altering experience for me.

During my time in the Philippines, I was reminded of some things that I thought I already knew, but had conveniently forgotten. For example, I was reminded of what a privilege and stroke of good fortune it was for me to have been born an American. My American citizenship has bestowed on me many rights and privileges that people in other places can only dream about. Not the least of these is the right to a free and appropriate education, which made it possible for me to become a Fulbright Scholar in the first place.

Another thing that I was reminded of was that although I have enjoyed all the rights and privileges of American citizenship throughout my lifetime, I have personally done little to earn my birthright. The rights and privileges of my American heritage are the legacy of countless, nameless, and faceless others who have gone before me, dedicated and courageous men and women who have struggled and suffered and sacrificed to build a free nation, where every man and woman is indeed created equal and every individual is guaranteed the right to life, liberty, and the pursuit of happiness.

I know it sounds corny, but being born an American is just about the most fortunate single event that can happen in the life of an average human being. It's too bad that it takes an unusual circumstance like living in a foreign country to be reminded of this simple truth. Since I returned from the Philippines, more than 15 years ago, I have kept my passport in my top drawer so I can see it and be reminded of how fortunate I am to be an American every morning when I get a clean pair of socks.

In addition to being reminded of some important things that I had conveniently forgotten, I learned some other valuable lessons while I was in the Philippines. I learned, for example, that although people in different parts of the world have different customs and habits, human beings are pretty much the same everywhere. The most basic hopes, dreams, and fears of human creatures are universal. No matter if you are in the Far East, Africa, or the midwestern United States, mothers and fathers still love their children more than their own lives; they worry about their ability to provide secure futures for them; and they struggle to provide them with the opportunity to build better lives than the ones they have experienced.

Perhaps the best thing about my extended stay in the Philippines was that it gave me the opportunity to slow down a little in a culture where the pace of life is much more relaxed and deliberate than it is in the United States. I found the slower pace frustrating at first, but revitalizing and revealing once I got adjusted to it. For the first time in years, I had enough time to take a deep breath, to think, and to observe the people and events that swirled around me. That's exactly what I was doing one day when a seemingly insignificant event provided me with an important insight.

I was leaning against the twisted trunk of an old coconut tree, waiting in the shade for the bus to Makati, where I lived at the time. Buses in metro Manila don't run on any particular schedule; they come when they come. I was fully prepared to wait for two minutes or two hours. After six months in the Philippines, I was finally starting to learn how to wait.

Across the road from the bus stop where I waited, a farmer and a carabao were plowing a rice paddy in the blazing noon-day sun. In the Philippines, carabao, or water buffalo as they are commonly known, are sometimes referred to as "Filipino tractors" because they are the only available alternative to mechanical farming devices in a largely undeveloped country.

As I watched, the ponderous beast swung his head from side to side in a rhythmic motion as he ambled along in knee-deep mud, straining against the weight of an ancient wooden plow. A small, wrinkled, brown-skinned farmer, barefooted and stripped to the waist, balanced precariously on the inclined sides of the rice paddy while skillfully steering the plow behind the plodding water buffalo. Down the east side of the small, square rice paddy, the two creatures moved in perfect tandem. They turned west, then south, then back east again, finally completing a circuit. When they had traveled the perimeter of the square in this manner several times, the water buffalo stopped dead in his tracks with no apparent sign from the farmer. The farmer jumped nimbly down into the rice paddy near the animal's head and, with the flat of his right foot, splashed cooling water against the great beast's sides. The brown-skinned little man moved deliberately up and down both sides of the panting animal, stopping only to repeat the splashing motion with first one foot and then the other. If a water buffalo can smile, then this one did as he clearly relished his brief respite from the stifling heat and his arduous labor.

I watched with interest as this scenario was repeated numerous times—the animal using his massive strength to pull the plow, the farmer agilely guiding it where it needed to go. The steady rhythm of the two creatures spinning out smaller and smaller circuits within the perimeter of the rice paddy was interrupted only by an occasional stop for the frail little man to splash the cooling water on his Filipino tractor. In a few weeks, young green rice plants would be waving in the soft, warm, tropical breeze, and after a time, there would be food for another year.

Transfixed, I stood and watched as the man and the animal worked together in this way. The perfect symbiosis represented by the farmer and the water buffalo, each contributing what he was capable of contributing to a common and essential task, created a simple but powerful image. Clearly, it would have been impossible for the farmer to pull the plow or for the beast to steer it where it needed to go. Each had to play the role that he was uniquely suited for, or the task could not be done, and ultimately there would be no life-sustaining food for either of them.

As we work and play and love our way through life, we find ourselves in so many different roles in our relationships with others. Sometimes it is our lot to pull the plow, to labor and strain against the harness to get to where we need to go. When we are struggling, mired up to our knees in the rich, thick mud of life, we pray that those who guide the plow will recognize and appreciate our efforts and demonstrate appropriate care and concern, much like the farmer did for the water buffalo. When it is our turn to guide the plow, we must likewise be sensitive to the needs of those whose lot it is to pull it and show our appreciation and compassion in ways both great and small. Only in this way can we hope to live well, accomplish much, and retain our humanity.

For the most part, teachers are the ones who pull the plows in the educational enterprise we refer to as schools. Day in and day out, they are mired in the rich, thick mud of teaching young people how to build lives that matter. But this should not always be the case. Sometimes, teachers are the ones who must guide the plow, and others (principals, media specialists, counselors, board members) are the ones who must pull it while taking their turn in the traces. It's not important who pulls or who guides. What is important is that we all work together to make the very best contribution to our common enterprise that we are capable of making and that we all recognize and appreciate the importance of the contributions that others make.

As a leader, are you taking care of your water buffalo? Do you understand the interdependence that binds every single person in an organization to every other person in that organization? Do you freely and frequently acknowledge that interdependence? Do you trust your colleagues enough to give up the reins when it is appropriate? Do you feel honored and gratified when you have an opportunity to pull the plow rather than to guide it?

The bus to Makati came and went that day, and still I waited in the shade of the coconut tree and watched the farmer and the water buffalo play out the same scenario over and over again. I was finally learning how to appreciate and even to enjoy the waiting.

Take Time to Reflect

What are some of the techniques that you employ to splash cooling water on your colleagues? Can you think of some others that you might use?

_____

_____

_____

_____

_____

_____

Why Am I Doing This?

I f the question, "What do I care about?" is the single most critical question that school leaders can ask themselves, then the question, "Why am I doing this?" may be a close second. Leaders make dozens and dozens of decisions every day. They are constantly struggling with what they should do in certain situations and how they should do it. Because of the sheer numbers of decisions that leaders must make and the limited time they have available in which to make them, it's easy, and even convenient, for leaders to forget why they are choosing one course of action over another and what the effect of their decisions might be on all the constituent groups and individuals they serve.

Despite the many decisions to be made and the crush of limited time available in which to make them, leaders need to realize that behind every decision is a motive or a reason. It's probably more accurate if we acknowledge that there are, in fact, numerous motives for most decisions that we make as leaders. These motives are varied in intensity and purpose and so intermingled that it is extremely difficult even to decipher them.

If we were to be completely honest with ourselves, then we would all be forced to admit that some of our motives for the decisions that we make are noble, whereas others are not so noble. Sometimes, we make a particular decision because we care about others and truly want to help someone in need. Other times, we may take a course of action not because it will necessarily help someone in need, but because we are expected to take that action in a given situation. For example, we may recommend a student for expulsion for bringing alcohol onto the school campus. Although we may not genuinely feel that expulsion is the best decision for this particular student, we are expected to enforce the district's policies, and those policies dictate the required decision. At other times, we make certain decisions because it is our job to do so. We develop a master schedule and give teachers their teaching assignments, arrange duty rosters, and so forth because these routine tasks have to done and it is our job to make the necessary decisions to see that they are.

A number of other motives for our decisions are not nearly so laudable as those I have mentioned thus far. In addition to wanting to help others or to meet the expectations of others or to carry out our job responsibilities, there are any number of not-so-nice motives for the decisions that leaders make. For example, sometimes we make decisions to assert our authority as leaders: We take a particular course of action because we can! By making a particular decision, we can feel superior, powerful, and in control of the situation. Sometimes, by choosing a specific course of action, we can put certain people in their places and reaffirm the pecking order. Other times, we may use decisions to punish people, teach them a lesson, or get even for some real or imagined transgression. At still other times, we may make a decision that will put someone in our debt, or perhaps we will decide an issue in a way that repays someone else to whom we feel indebted. All these not-so-nice motives are lurking in the shadows, ready to creep into the decisions of leaders who are not vigilant enough to ask themselves the critical question "Why am I doing this?" As Greenleaf (1996) has noted, "A capable supervisor is necessarily a student of motives, not necessarily versed in the jargon of the professionals but nevertheless is ever watchful of the effect of each order, suggestion, or word of advice on each individual" (p. 180).

In my role as a high school principal, I always regarded myself as being extremely student oriented. I felt it was my sacred duty to be a powerful and outspoken advocate for the young people in our school and to use my position and the authority that went with it in every way possible to see that the interests of children were promoted and protected. As might be expected, I had lots of opportunities to test my resolve in my efforts to be an effective advocate for children.

One afternoon in the late spring, the parents of one of the students in our school came to my office to meet with me. Although I had never met either Mr. or Mrs. Curry, I did know their son, Richard, who was a member of the senior class. I could tell instantly that the Currys were upset, and it didn't take them long to explain why. They told me that Richard was experiencing a personal crisis and they had reached the end of their rope in their efforts to deal with it.

Mr. Curry briefly recounted for me Richard's sterling record as a high school student. He told me that Richard had never made a grade lower than a B in his entire school career and had been tapped into the National Honor Society when he was a sophomore. Because of his success on the PSAT, Richard had been named a Merit Scholar semifinalist the previous fall. In addition to his academic prowess, Richard had been actively involved in student life, having been a member of student government for several years in addition to serving as the coeditor of the yearbook during his junior year. As the result of his outstanding academic achievement coupled with his record of student leadership, Richard's family had recently been notified that he was a finalist for a prestigious scholarship at an Ivy League college. But the Currys were terrified that all this success was about to blow up in their faces.

Mrs. Curry told me that her son's behavior had recently become erratic. Richard, who had always been outgoing and friendly, had suddenly become sullen and moody. He had begun to display frequent fits of anger, during which he smashed objects in his room and cried uncontrollably. Richard's old friends had stopped coming around to the house, and his parents suspected that his new friends were into drugs. In their desperation to help their son, the Currys had consulted a psychiatrist, who confirmed their own feelings that Richard was suffering from a deep depression. Although Richard was being treated for depression and his parents were beginning to see some positive results of the treatment, there was a pressing problem that they needed my help in resolving.

Several weeks before my meeting with the Currys, their son had skipped school on the day that an important physics examination was given. Because Richard had received an unexcused absence for that day, the physics teacher had refused to allow Richard to make up his examination and had instead given him a grade of zero. The zero dropped Richard's grade in physics from an A- to a D for the semester. Mr. Curry explained to me that the D in physics was a much more serious problem than might ordinarily be the case because it would probably disqualify Richard from further consideration for his pending scholarship at the Ivy League college and negate all the years of hard work that he had put in to get himself to this point in his academic career. To complicate the situation further, the psychiatrist had warned the Currys that in his professional judgment, their son might be suicidal, and he advised them that it was critical that Richard not be subjected to any undue stress or pressure at this particular time in his life. With that explanation, the Currys asked me to please intercede with the teacher on behalf of their son and see that he received an opportunity to make up the examination.

I was deeply touched by the Currys' story. I immediately told them not to worry. I promised that I would talk with the teacher as soon as I possibly could, and I assured these deeply troubled parents that the teacher, Mr. Kidd, would provide their son with an opportunity to make up the missed examination and redeem his grade. I got the shock of my professional life when I went to see Mr. Kidd.

When I promised Mr. and Mrs. Curry that I would intercede on behalf of their son, I assumed that there was only one proper course of action to take in this situation, and that was to allow Richard to make up the examination. Clearly, this decision was in the student's best interest, and I felt it was my responsibility to see that the school acted in this interest. Furthermore, I assumed that Mr. Kidd would see it that way too and that once I explained the situation to him, the matter would be quickly and neatly resolved. When I made what I thought was a reasonable request to Mr. Kidd that Richard be allowed to make up the examination and perhaps be penalized a letter grade or so for his failure to take it at the scheduled time, I was met with a polite but stern refusal. Mr. Kidd told me in no uncertain terms that the rules did not allow students to make up work for days on which they received unexcused absences and that he was going to enforce the rules come hell or high water!

When Mr. Kidd responded to me in this way, I realized that I would have to share some of the important details of this particular situation so that he could understand that this situation was indeed unique and justified breaking (or at least bending) the rules. But I didn't tell him that Richard might be suicidal, because the parents had asked me not to reveal this particular detail unless it was absolutely unavoidable. So, I shared some of the other important details of the situation with Mr. Kidd, such as Richard's sterling record and potential scholarship.

The physics teacher remained intractable in his position, however. He assured me that he had no intention of bowing to parental pressure and violating his principles when it came to assigning grades to his students, no matter what the circumstances. At that point, I knew that I had to play my ace card. I told Mr. Kidd about the mental state of his student, and I shared my feelings that perhaps Richard would do something foolish if he were not allowed to make up the examination.

I was astonished when Mr. Kidd was unmoved by my argument. He told me, "Look, stop bothering me about this! I've already told you that I'm not going to allow Richard to make up the examination!" With that declaration, I moved swiftly into my power mode. "I'm not asking you any longer," I said. "I'm telling you! You will arrange for him to make up the examination!"

Richard made up the examination, although I don't recall whether or not he received his scholarship. But I do know that he graduated and went off to college somewhere, and I'm fairly certain that he didn't take his own life, because I would have read about it in the newspaper. In addition to all these consequences of my decision to allow Richard to make up his physics exam, there was one additional important consequence. I destroyed the professional relationship that I had previously enjoyed with the physics teacher. Because of this one disagreement and the way in which I handled it, I was never again able to win his support.

I've told myself many times over the years that I made the right decision. After all, the student was given an opportunity to correct a mistake he had made, and he didn't take drastic action to end his life. I have consoled myself for the loss of the physics teacher's support with the question "What else could I have done in a situation like this where the stakes were impossibly high?"

When I am really honest with myself and I am forced to ask myself the question, "Why did I do this?" I see a different side to the situation. When I started out to resolve the problem, my motives were reasonably pure. I was genuinely concerned for Richard's welfare. I wanted to help him, and I wanted to help his troubled parents.

But as the situation evolved, my pure motives got tangled up with some not-so-pure motives. When the teacher resisted my attempts to resolve the problem in the way I thought it should be resolved, I began to feel that my authority was being challenged and that my leadership and my professional judgment were being called into question. At some point in the exchange between myself and Mr. Kidd, my motives shifted from wanting to help Richard and his parents to wanting to put this defiant teacher in his place, to show him who was boss, and to reaffirm my power as the leader in the school. When I'm being completely honest with myself, I also admit that I wasn't about to let a teacher show me up in the community. In my heart of hearts, I had no intention of having Richard's parents telling all their friends and neighbors that I didn't keep my word to them and I allowed a teacher to walk all over me and their son.

Although I still feel that it was the correct decision to allow Richard to make up his examination, I hope that I could arrive at that decision in a different manner if confronted with a similar situation today. I would involve the teacher from the beginning and earnestly seek his or her advice and counsel. I now realize that I usurped the teacher's authority and called his professionalism into question by excluding him from the decision-making process. It is little wonder he resisted me as strongly as he did. If I were a principal today, I would make sure that I had a mechanism such as an appeals committee, composed of teachers and other staff members, for deciding when to make exceptions to established policy. Most of all, I would ask myself, "Why am I doing this?" so that I could avoid taking significant actions for the wrong reasons.

The most important lesson here is for school leaders to realize that there are motives for almost every action taken. These motives vary in intensity and purpose and can shift dramatically at a moment's notice. Some of these motives are extremely positive, whereas others are equally negative. If we are truly committed to fulfilling our responsibilities to those we lead, it is imperative that we take the time to examine our motives for our actions in a timely manner.

Examining one's motives is vital to effective leadership, because human beings are closely attuned to the motives that underlie the actions of others.

Most people seem to be able to sense intuitively whether those in leadership roles are doing what they are doing for the right reasons or the wrong reasons. If the motives underlying the actions of leaders are perceived by others as being positive, then people will support leaders in their actions and assist them in their efforts to lead. On the other hand, if the motives underlying a leader's actions are judged by others to be negative, then people will resist those actions and challenge the authority of the leader at every opportunity.

Leaders must strive to become reflective in the sense that they think about and closely study both their thoughts and deeds related to providing leadership for others. They need to dissect their actions by constantly asking questions such as the following:

1. What was the nature of the problem that I was attempting to solve?

2. What actions did I take?

3. What were the good and bad results of those actions?

4. What would I do differently if I had to do it all over again?

5. Can I in some way make up for the mistakes that I have made or the harm that I have caused others?

Most important, leaders need to ask themselves that critical question, "Why am I doing this?" as often as they possibly can. If you as a leader ask yourself this question and you don't like the answer you receive, then you almost certainly need to change your behavior or at least rearrange your priorities. On the other hand, if you find that you are gratified by the answer you receive, then chances are that others will be gratified as well, and they will demonstrate their gratification by trusting you enough to allow you to lead. In the words of Mark Twain, "Always do right—this will gratify some people and astonish the rest."

Take Time to Reflect

Try to recall a decision you made recently while acting in some sort of leadership role (e.g., formal work role, parenting role, informal group leader, etc.). Why did you make the particular decision that you made? Were there both positive and negative motives underlying the decision? What were some of these motives, both positive and negative?

_____

_____

_____

_____

_____

_____

_____

_____

_____

_____

_____

_____

_____

_____

_____

_____

_____

_____

_____

_____

_____

_____

_____

_____

_____

_____

Who's the King
or Queen of the Jungle?

I t must have been about twenty-five years ago that I heard a story about status and what can happen to someone who takes his or her place in the pecking order too seriously. The story went something like this.

One morning a big, old African lion awoke from his night's sleep feeling especially pleased with himself. Game had been plentiful of late, his hunts had been unusually successful, and he was growing stronger and fatter with each passing day. The lion slowly stretched and scratched a little itch on the back of his neck with one huge paw. He yawned a mighty yawn that reached clear to the depths of his aristocratic soul, and shook his great head from side to side in an effort to throw off the effects of his long, pleasant slumber.

While he was leisurely shaking his head in this way and rolling his long mane from side to side, he suddenly realized that he was thirsty. So, the lion decided that he would take a stroll down to the nearby water hole and get a nice cool drink of water to relieve his thirst. "Yes," he said to himself. "That will be the perfect way for me to start my day."

The lion gave his great, sleepy head one last big shake to get the cobwebs out and sauntered on down to the white sandy beach at the edge of the water hole to get his drink. It was a pleasantly cool morning, the sun was shining brightly through the trees, birds were singing sweet songs all around him, and the air smelled fresh and clean. The lion decided that this day was indeed going to be a glorious day!

When the mighty beast arrived at the water hole, he began to drink rapidly at first, then more slowly and leisurely as he felt his thirst subside. As the lion drank the sweet, cool water, he couldn't help but notice his reflection staring back at him from the surface of the crystal clear pool.

He marveled at his grand countenance. He admired his many regal assets. He was greatly pleased as he surveyed his fierce, long, white teeth; his piercing golden eyes; his rich, thick, full mane; and the tight mounds of huge muscles that rippled throughout his mighty chest.

Carefully studying his reflection in this way, it was impossible for the lion not to notice that he was truly a magnificent creature. But even while he was viewing the evidence of what a remarkable animal he was, unpleasant thoughts began to creep into his psyche and intrude on his feelings of contentment. Deep in the inner recesses of his mind, the lion wondered if all the other animals realized what a wonderful and magnificent creature he was. Did they freely acknowledge that he, the mighty lion, was the king of all the beasts? The lion couldn't allow his glorious day to be ruined by such negative and distressing thoughts. He decided that he would find out right away just how the other animals felt and thereby put the matter to rest once and for all.

The lion took one last admiring look at his reflection in the water, then turned and stalked into the jungle. There was a sense of purpose in his steps. He was going to remind the other animals that he, and he alone, was the king of the jungle. The first animal he met on his foray into the jungle was an unfortunate monkey, who was distracted by his efforts to break open a coconut on a rock and consequently had not noticed the lion's approach. Before he knew it, the lion had grabbed him around his neck in a viselike grip. The lion pulled the monkey up against him in a fearful embrace. "Foolish little monkey!" he bellowed. "Who is the king of the jungle?" Though frightened out of his wits, the monkey didn't hesitate in his reply. "Why you are, mighty lion. You are the king of the jungle." "That's right, and just be sure you don't forget it!" said the lion with a satisfied little snort.

The lion released the frightened monkey and moved deeper into the jungle. There, he saw a giraffe eating leaves from the top of a Banyan tree. The lion got a running start, leaped up high into the air, and grabbed the giraffe around the neck with his saberlike claws while yanking the giraffe's head down to the ground in one smooth, powerful motion. The lion stared with a terrible intensity into the terrified, soft, brown eyes of the giraffe. "Answer this question correctly, and I might even decide to let you live, you big gawky freak," said the lion. "Who is the king of the jungle?" The giraffe's knees were shaking so hard he could barely stand, much less speak. It was only by summoning all his inner strength that the gentle giant was able to reply in a barely audible whisper, "Why you are sir— everyone knows that you are the king of the jungle." "Say it again, and this time say it louder!" demanded the lion. "Oh, mighty lion, please don't kill me! You are the king of the beasts. Everyone knows that you are the king of the beasts," responded the giraffe. "That's absolutely correct!" said the lion. "I am the king of the beasts!" He released the giraffe, while cautioning him that he'd better not forget for a single moment that he, the mighty lion, was the one and only king.

Although the lion was feeling quite a bit better about himself by this time, he decided that he required just a little more assurance. As fate would have it, the next animal that the king of the beasts encountered was an old bull elephant, who was busy scratching his backside against a convenient coconut tree. The lion surveyed the elephant and immediately made the decision that this would be the perfect confirmation of his superiority throughout the entire animal kingdom. The lion marched defiantly up to the old elephant, who had his eyes closed and was clearly enjoying himself, rhythmically moving his ample backside to and fro against the coconut tree in a kind of soothing dance. The lion grabbed the elephant by the trunk and jerked the great beast's head in a violent motion down to a place where the two animals were at eye level. The mighty lion roared as loudly as he could directly into the old elephant's ear, "Hey, you big, fat, dumb jerk! Who's the king of the beasts?" For a fleeting moment, genuine surprise was reflected in the elephant's squinty little eyes. Unfortunately for the king of the beasts, that look of surprise was quickly replaced by a look of rage. Before the lion could realize what was happening to him, the bull elephant had wrapped his powerful trunk tightly around the big cat's midsection. He twirled the lion around and around over his huge, gray head until the lion was totally disoriented. Then the elephant pounded the lion against the coconut tree until the lion's body was one giant bruise. Finally satisfied that he had punished the lion sufficiently, the elephant threw the king of the beasts unceremoniously to the ground in a big heap.

The elephant returned to scratching himself on his favorite coconut tree, while the stunned lion slowly staggered to his feet and dusted himself off. He surveyed the elephant with a confused look on his regal face and muttered softly, "Well, you don't have to get mad just because you don't know the answer."

How easy it is for someone in a leadership role to feel like the king of the jungle. Unless they are careful, leaders can overvalue the trappings that frequently go hand in hand with rank. Bigger offices, travel budgets, personal secretaries, designated parking spaces, and increased compensation can all conspire to tell the leader that he or she is extra special and perhaps should even be valued above others in the organization. When subordinates actively seek the leader's counsel and defer to the leader's judgment in all matters great and small, it's easy for the leader to lose perspective and begin to believe that he or she may even be a king or queen of the jungle.

But leaders can never forget that schools are not jungles—at least they shouldn't be! On the contrary, schools must be nurturing and caring places where people are willing to make themselves vulnerable so that they as well as others can experience intellectual, social, and emotional growth. Even the most cynical among us would be forced to agree that one can't do these things well in a junglelike environment.

Leadership is never about ruling others; leadership is about serving others.

Max De Pree (1989) perhaps puts it best when he says that the art of leadership is "liberating people to do what is required of them in the most effective and humane way possible" (p. xx). In this way, leaders are, in fact, "servants" of their followers, in that they remove the obstacles that prevent their followers from working to the best of their abilities. Force, fear, and intimidation are not the least bit liberating.

People cannot function as workers or learners at their maximum potential when they can't feel safe and free from external threats. It is the leader's responsibility to help all those in the organization to be safe and to feel safe—to liberate them to do what is required of them in the most effective and humane way possible!

As far as rank and status are concerned, they are relatively meaningless. The leader can serve as the king or queen of the jungle only at the pleasure of all those who are served. As soon as the leader forgets this important lesson, it's just a matter of time until he or she receives a painful reminder. Leaders must never forget that the strongest people of all are also the most gentle: The strength of their convictions coupled with their caring natures gives them an inner strength that doesn't require external confirmation. Be careful, oh ye mighty lions, there is a whole herd of elephants waiting for you out there!

Take Time to Reflect

Lions are able to rule the jungle because they are fearsome and powerful creatures and most of the other animals are in no position to challenge them. Some individuals in leadership roles rule their respective organizations as if they were lions.

Their coworkers allow them to rule because, like the other jungle creatures, they are also not in positions to challenge them. If you could choose to be an animal in your own "organizational jungle," what animal would you choose to be and how would that translate into your leadership style?

_____

_____

_____

_____

_____

_____

_____

_____

_____

_____

_____

_____

_____

_____

_____

_____

_____

_____

_____

_____

_____

_____

_____

Honey, Do These Pants Make Me Look Fat?

U p until this point, the questions posed to the reader have been relatively easy. But prepare yourself, because that's about to change. "Honey, do these pants make me look fat?" is precisely the kind of question that has the potential to make you place your hands over your ears and run out of the room screaming. This is a question that no sane person ever wants to answer.

What makes this question so impossible? The question is impossible because by choosing an answer, we are forced to also choose between two competing outcomes that are both highly desirable. On one hand, most of us value the truth, and even if the truth is not particularly pretty, it's still the truth. So, if we are inclined to answer truthfully, the response might go something like this: "Fat's not the word! Those pants make you look enormous!" (We're being really truthful in this instance.) By answering truthfully, we are able to preserve our integrity, but at the same time, we risk hurting the feelings of someone we care for a great deal, and in the process, we may even damage an important relationship. So, in this instance, we might disdain the truth and choose an answer that is decidedly short on honesty but long on sensitivity, such as, "Wow! Sweetheart! You look absolutely fabulous in those pants! In fact, I believe they are slimming on you!" (We're being really sensitive here.) This answer doesn't earn any points for integrity, but it promotes warm fuzzy feelings and preserves harmony in an important relationship.

So, what's the best answer to, "Honey, do these pants make me look fat?" I suppose that depends on a lot of variables that are highly idiosyncratic to each particular situation. When we can, most of us probably frame an answer somewhere in the middle of the two extremes I have proposed above: "Sweetheart, I'm such a poor judge of fashion. All I know is that you look beautiful to me no matter what you are wearing!" With this answer, we try to preserve a little integrity balanced with a bit of compassion—and then ask for forgiveness when we say our prayers at the end of the day. (I suppose that I should admit that answers of this nature have made it possible for my wife and me to stay happily married for thirty-five years. She frequently tells me what I want to hear!)

Unfortunately, many times there is no middle ground when making decisions in an organizational setting. We must choose one outcome or the other, because to compromise would result in the loss of both desirable outcomes. In the never-ending battle to build and maintain ethical and caring organizations, the challenge isn't related so much to the constant struggle to decide between right and wrong. The choices are relatively easy in those instances where we are able to differentiate right from wrong; we simply choose right. However, as illustrated in the example above, the more difficult ethical challenge involves making choices between two mutually exclusive outcomes, both of which are highly desirable. These choices between right and right create moral dilemmas for caring leaders.

When I was serving as a school principal, I always took responsibility for the preparation of the master schedule. I reserved this responsibility for myself because I was pretty well convinced that a smoothly functioning school revolved around a well-conceived master schedule. Besides, I was a certified control freak at that time in my life, and I didn't have the capacity to trust this task to anyone else. So each spring, I would meet with each of the department chairs in turn, in the big conference room located at the rear of the administrative suite. There, we would arrange and rearrange courses on a big pegboard until we arrived at the master schedule we felt would work best for our students, our teachers, and ultimately, our school.

One year, we hired a new language arts teacher who had just completed an MA degree in American Literature. Because Jane was a new teacher and had a real strength in the area, the chair of the Language Arts department and I agreed that her teaching assignment should include several sections of American Literature. The only problem with this decision was that Neal, one of the most senior teachers on the staff, had traditionally taught all the sections of American Lit for as long as anyone could remember. Neal was more than a little upset when the final version of the master schedule was posted prior to student registration for the coming year.

In fact, when Neal reviewed the schedule, he couldn't believe his eyes. Who was this "Jane person" who was intruding on his domain? As soon as he recovered enough from the shock of seeing several sections of *his course* next to someone else's name, he made straight for my office. Neal was pretty intense when he stormed into the room. As I remember it, smoke was billowing out of both ears. He walked right up to my desk and pounded on it with his fist for emphasis. "Why are you giving *my course* to someone else?" he demanded to know. "Well, Neal," I said, "we didn't give 'your course' to someone else. We made a decision to divide the American Literature sections between you and Jane." "Oh no you don't!" Neal shouted. "I am the American Literature teacher in this school! I teach all the sections of American Literature!"

I did my best to explain our reasoning for splitting the American Literature sections. I told Neal that because Jane was new to the teaching profession, we needed to do all that we could to provide her with an assignment that would help to assure her a successful first-year experience. I also explained that as a veteran teacher, we felt that Neal could easily make the needed adjustments to handle a more varied teaching assignment than he had been given in the past. "Besides," I told him, "it's good to try something new once in a while. It helps keeps you fresh."

But Neal didn't want to be fresh! He wanted to teach five sections of American Literature! He persisted, and insisted that I change his teaching assignment. Finally, when he wasn't able to get the answer he wanted from me, he played his trump card. "I thought you were my friend," he said. "I am your friend, Neal," I assured him. "But I'm also the principal of the school, and I have to make the decisions that I feel are best for our students and our school." With that, Neal turned on his heel and left my office. Thankfully, a week or so later, he stopped by the office again to let me know that although he still preferred to teach all the sections of American Literature, he understood the decision and was already working to prepare for his new assignment.

Putting aside the fact that I had handled the situation poorly in that I hadn't anticipated such a negative reaction from Neal and therefore hadn't made an effort to win him over before making the decision public, the question remained: Was this decision the right decision? There were, of course, several desirable and undesirable outcomes on both sides of this issue. If I had let Neal have all the American Literature sections, he would no doubt have been pleased with his assignment. By honoring Neal's preference over the needs of a first-year teacher, I could have demonstrated my respect for seniority among the teaching staff, and Neal would have continued to think of me as a loyal, trustworthy, and caring friend. However, had I made that choice, I would have also done a disservice to our new teacher, Jane, by giving her an assignment that didn't play to her strengths. In doing so, I would have also ignored my responsibility to our students to give them the best teacher possible in every classroom, because Jane was unquestionably the better prepared of the two to teach American Literature despite Neal's rather impressive record of longevity as *the teacher* of the course.

Again, it's not a simple question of right versus wrong. The kinds of dilemmas that school leaders face as they make hundreds of routine and not-so-routine decisions on a daily basis invariably pit a wide range of values against each other. And if leaders don't know the relative place of competing values in their own personal value systems, then they are vulnerable to the urge to substitute others' values in place of their own when the going gets a little rough. The choice to divide the American Literature sections between Neal and Jane was a relatively simple decision, but many other choices facing school leaders every day are anything but simple. For example, should principals always support the teachers when they have issues with students or parents? Does the principal continue to support the teacher in these issues even when the teacher is clearly wrong?

The most difficult decisions force leaders to choose not between right and wrong, but between right and right. As Badaracco (1997) has pointed out, in such circumstances, it is extremely difficult for leaders to know

> What to do when one clear right thing must be left undone in order to do another or when doing the right thing requires doing something wrong. . . . The right versus right problems typically involve choices between two or more courses of action, each of which is a complicated bundle of ethical responsibilities, personal commitments, moral hazards and practical pressures and constraints. (p. 6)

If we can think of these moral dilemmas as caused by a whole series of choices of right versus right, then a lengthy list of considerations presents itself. When it comes to decisions between right and right, we must recognize that there is typically no black and white, but plenty of gray. For example, when deciding an issue of right versus right, rather than asking ourselves if a particular course of action is right or wrong, we might do well to ask ourselves whether the course of action taken will be fair to all concerned, will be just, personally satisfying, self-promoting, culturally acceptable, or individually acceptable. We may also want to question whether or not the decision or action will produce the greatest utility, minimize harm, violate a written or unwritten contract, meet an obligation, or violate a spoken or unspoken promise. We may even need to decide whether, if given the opportunity, we would take the same action again; or we might do well to ponder the likelihood of our peers taking the same action if they were presented with a similar set of circumstances. For most right versus right decisions, some of the answers to the series of questions and considerations posed above will be ethically desirable, whereas others will be ethically undesirable. Regardless of the course of action taken, "Some right thing must be left undone in order to do another right thing or doing the right thing will require doing something else wrong."

Badaracco (1997) warns all those who would attempt to lead that right versus right decisions reveal values, test commitment, and shape the future of the organization. Because so many values are in competition with each other, leaders are forced to prioritize their values (and the values of their organizations) when faced with making right versus right decisions. This prioritization process will test the leader's commitment to a value system, because many times the choices are extremely difficult. Making these difficult choices lets everyone know whether a leader can "walk the talk" when put to the test. Badaracco cautions that right versus right decisions are extremely critical to the long-term welfare of an organization because they have the capacity to shape the future of that organization by setting parameters for how future decisions are likely to be made. This phenomenon, which Badaracco has termed "shadowing forward," often leads to what he calls "defining moments" (p. 6) in the life of the leader and the organization and serve as "crucibles of character" (p. 4) as they test and mold the character of the leader.

So, what is right? Are there instances when friendship or loyalty can trump responsibility? Does integrity rank higher on the values meter than seniority? When making decisions, is respect for the individual a more important consideration than the consequences of that decision to the organization? And finally, be honest: "Do these pants make me look fat?"

Take Time to Reflect

Think of an occasion when you had to make a "right versus right" decision. What was the nature of the decision? What values were in competition? Why did you decide in the way that you decided? If you had it to do again, would you make the same decision today? Why or why not?

_____

_____

_____

_____

_____

_____

_____

_____

_____

_____

_____

_____

_____

What Does It Mean to Be a Teacher?

W hen I landed my first job as a teacher, I was one of two first-year teachers hired to teach in the school that year. Because I was a new teacher and the school was small and rural, my teaching assignment was challenging, to say the least. I was assigned to teach seventh-, eighth-, ninth-, and tenth-grade English, with an additional class assignment of teaching reading to all the seventh- and eighth-grade students who were two or more years below grade level in reading. There weren't enough classrooms for all the teachers in the school, so I had the misfortune to be designated as a floating teacher and was required to move from classroom to classroom during the course of the day to meet my classes. Unfortunately, there were no empty classrooms available for two of my English classes, and consequently those two classes were assigned to meet in the auditorium. There were no blackboards or lapboards, and the auditorium wasn't heated. The fact that the auditorium wasn't heated may not seem like a big problem because the school was in Florida, but I can assure you that it gets cold in northern Florida in the winter in an unheated auditorium. On the coldest days, I would move my classes outside to the football stadium, where the kids could usually find a place out of the wind and take advantage of the warmth of the sunlight.

I will never forget what those first few weeks of teaching were like. There I was, a first-year teacher with five different preparations, floating from class to class, teaching two periods in an unheated auditorium. My principal had also scheduled me for first-period planning and assigned me to a desk in the main office area. I suppose I was pretty naive, because it took me the better part of a month to realize that the principal had assigned me to that time in the office so that he could conveniently dispatch me to cover the first-period classes of teachers who were late to school or called in sick at the last minute. As I remember it, I didn't take advantage of too many planning periods during my first semester as a teacher.

The icing on the cake during that first year was the sixth-period reading class: forty-two seventh and eighth graders who were two or more years below grade level in reading! There were only twenty-six desks in Mrs. Peterson's classroom, where I was assigned to teach my reading students. I had all the desks filled with students; two students were assigned to sit in each of the three window boxes, and the rest were scattered about on the floor at my feet. I remember how much I wished that I had had some training in how to teach reading or at least some appropriate materials that I could use with the class.

It was plain bad luck that Judd was a member of my sixth-period reading class as well as being a student in my eighth-grade English class, which met earlier in the day. I can still see Judd's face if I close my eyes and concentrate. Judd bore a strong physical resemblance to the character "Zero" in the Beetle Bailey comic strips. But compared to Judd, Zero was a real sweetheart, as well as a near genius. I asked myself on many occasions, "Did Judd really have it in for me, or was he simply a stone-age ADD kid?" Whatever the case, Judd made my life miserable every school day.

After numerous referrals to the office, Judd was finally suspended from school, and the assistant principal arranged for Judd's mother to come in for a parent conference. That conference was an epiphany for me! When we had taken our respective seats for the conference, the first words out of the mother's mouth were, "If you people can't handle Judd here at school, then how in the hell do you expect me to handle him at home?" Although I was temporarily stunned by her words, it was at that precise moment that I knew that this "teaching thing" was going to be a lot more difficult than I had ever imagined it would be.

If I live to be a very old man with a long white beard, I will never forget what those first few weeks of teaching were like! I will always remember just how ill prepared I was to meet the challenges that went with the territory, how isolated I was from my colleagues, how inadequate I felt every day when I walked into that little rural schoolhouse, and how insensitive, uncaring, and unprofessional my "school leader" was to give me a teaching assignment that would have defeated a more seasoned teacher. I vowed then that if I ever had the opportunity to lead a school, I would make sure that no teacher in that school would ever experience what I experienced those first few weeks and months as a teacher. To this day, I have tried faithfully to keep that vow.

School leaders must never forget that teaching is the real business of schools, and they must always hold close to their hearts what it means to be a teacher. I find it distressing that the general public has little respect for what it means to be a teacher, but I find it devastating for school leaders to fail to realize or to forget the high level of sacrifice, dedication, and commitment required to be an effective classroom teacher. Apart from all those first-year teachers who are bound to struggle while they are learning to be teachers, there are all those teachers who grind it out day after day to serve their students' needs to the best of their abilities: for example, the English teacher who assigns multiple writing experiences for her students and spends hours at night and on weekends writing feedback to them. What about the advanced placement history teacher who has to fight hard for every dime to buy supplemental texts for his students? We must not forget teachers who are also parents and committed to attending their own children's football or soccer games, plays, or musical performances, or the teachers who seek to restore the balance in their own lives by participating in community theater, community affairs, or charitable organizations.

Teachers are among the most highly represented occupational groups in volunteer community organizations and activities. It is not unusual for an average teacher to spend about twelve hours a day, in and out of the classroom, on activities directly related to teaching and school.

When I was preparing to write this book, I made the mistake of describing "caring teachers" to a colleague in terms that she did not appreciate. I described caring teachers as "the ones who volunteer when there is something to be done and no one wants to do it . . . the ones who come to school early and leave late . . . their chief concern is not with taking care of their own personal needs, but with doing more for others."

My colleague, who had devoted the majority of her professional life to teaching, jumped down my throat. She verbally slammed me to the floor and wouldn't let me up until I cried "uncle." I've never heard a more eloquent description of the demands on the life of a caring and committed professional teacher:

> You have described a person who does not have a balanced life, or who is single and has nothing else to do. I know this teacher all too well—I am she. I went to school at 6:00 a.m. and stayed until 5:00 p.m., and then came back at night for PTA. I was the main liaison with parents for the school. I was chair of most schoolwide committees. I took the lead in writing curriculum. I was a successful grantwriter. . . . Beginning in 1982, I led the restructuring efforts, not just for my school, but for the entire district. I was a mentor teacher to new

and marginal teachers. I made sure that if one of my 150 students was in any school event—athletic or other performance—I attended the performance and made a point of commenting on it to the student in class the next day. I was assistant principal for curriculum and instruction for two years, but it involved even more "extra duty" and took me away from the teaching and interaction with students that I so dearly loved. So I asked for a classroom assignment again. Education was (and is) my passion! I was acknowledged by the school board, administration, parents, and teachers alike as the consummate professional. And I did this while raising four children (the last of whom is sixteen and a senior in high school) and being there for my husband, who spent the last eleven years of his life in a constant battle with lymphoma. I loved teaching, and I wouldn't give up a day of my teaching experience—but I would *never* do it again. When you care that much, teaching can suck up every minute of your life and still demand more. I definitely did not lead a balanced life, and in my commitment to meet the needs of everyone else in my life, there was no time to ever meet my own needs. In looking back on my career and wondering if my efforts mattered, I feel somewhat like Simon Bolivar, who, on his deathbed, was asked to look back on his life and reflect on how he felt about all he had done for his people. Bolivar responded that he felt like he had been plowing the ocean. . . . Still, I have no regrets; life is about making choices, and I found gratification and fulfillment in how I chose to spend my time in my first career.

I want to take this opportunity to thank my colleague for setting me straight in terms of what it means to be a caring teacher. And I want to thank her for reminding me that there are many teachers out there who give everything they have for their students every single day they walk into a classroom—and still the profession demands that they give more. She forced me to realize that school leaders must occasionally protect teachers who care too much from themselves.

Do you remember what it was like to be a beginning teacher? If you're not presently a teacher, do you remember what it was like to be one? Do you still appreciate on a daily basis the incredible demands that come with being a highly committed and caring teacher? Do you know highly committed and caring teachers in your own schools like the one my colleague described? Are you doing everything in your power not only to appreciate them, but to save them from themselves if need be? School leaders can never forget what it means to be a teacher.

Take Time to Reflect

Do you have vivid memories of your first year as a teacher? What was that experience like for you? If you could go back and alter that experience in some way, how would you make it different?

_____

_____

_____

_____

_____

_____

_____

_____

_____

_____

Can You Just Call
Me Willie, Mrs. Peterson?

Early in my teaching career, I had the opportunity to attend the state convention of the Florida Education Association in Miami as a delegate. It was a tremendously exciting experience for a small-town boy like me. At that point in my life, I didn't expect to find myself in the "magic city," taking part in an important professional meeting. The experience was particularly memorable because we also had a candidate from our local school district running for president of the association. The opportunity to campaign for her made the experience that much more exciting. Whoever was managing our candidate's campaign came up with a ladybug theme as a way to establish an identity for our candidate (the other candidate was a male). So, we all went around Miami for the better part of a week sporting ladybug vests and top hats. When I think back to how silly we all looked, it's no wonder our candidate was soundly defeated.

Although it's been almost thirty-five years since I took part in that convention, a singular, seemingly insignificant event still stands out in my mind. The event occurred during a general session, when the platform of the association was being debated among the delegates. There was something in the platform related to race. I don't remember the exact nature of the provision. I just remember the debate it stirred and the actions of a group of black delegates from southern Florida. As the provision was being debated, the discussion became more and more heated. A leader of the black delegates had the floor. He turned his head slowly and looked disdainfully around the room at the sea of white faces staring back at him. Finally, he proclaimed, while shaking his finger accusingly, "The problem with you people is that you don't know what it's like to be black!" With that damning pronouncement, he turned and strode defiantly out of the convention hall, followed closely by every black person in the room.

I was shocked! I was stunned! I was insulted! It wasn't the hasty departure of the black delegates that shocked, stunned, and insulted me. It was the charge leveled against me and all the other white delegates in the room that day, that we didn't know what it was like to be black—that we didn't even have the basic human capacity to recognize and appreciate the plight of our fellow black teachers. As the black delegates silently filed out of the auditorium, I thought to myself, "Just who the hell does he think he is? We're (my white brothers and sisters) all bright, educated, sensitive people. We weren't born yesterday. It's not like we don't even know any black people—why most of us even have black friends! How does he come off telling us we 'don't know what it's like to be black?' Of course we know what it's like to be black!"

Today, I'm a little embarrassed that I reacted as I did to that black leader's words those many years ago. Now I realize just how right he was: I didn't have a clue as to what it was like to be black.

I grew up in a small town in northeast Florida during the 1950s and 60s. Although I completed my formal public school education about ten years after *Brown v. Board of Education* (1954), I never went to school with a black child. What's more, I never really knew any black people while I was growing up. I can't recall ever having a discussion or even a polite conversation with a black person until I joined the Navy after graduation from high school in 1963.

Everything in my town was separate for blacks and whites, from water fountains to restrooms to restaurants to schools—separate, but certainly not equal. Blacks were restricted to the balcony seats at the local movie theater, they were forced to ride in the back of city buses, and their neighborhoods were confined to several pockets in the poorer sections of the town. Where black people lived was about the only thing I had in common with them.

My mother had divorced my father when I was still a small child. She worked as a waitress at a restaurant in town, and the lack of financial resources had forced her to move with my sister and me to live with my grandmother in a small, wood-frame house without indoor plumbing on the west side of town. The street where I lived butted up against a black neighborhood. I saw black people passing by on the street each day, going and coming, carrying on the business of living, but I never spoke a word to them or acknowledged their existence in any way. I was afraid of black people when I was a small child.

When I was growing up, everything that I thought I knew about race and social class I learned from my grandmother and my uncles, aunts, and cousins. They were the most significant people in my small world. The word *nigger* was frequently used by those around me to denote black people. It sounds ridiculous to me now, but as a small child, I had no idea that the term was derogatory. Nigger was used so often, so casually, and without rancor in a matter-of-fact way that I thought the term was merely descriptive, like New Yorker, or South American, or Baptist.

When I was three or four, I would spend most Saturday afternoons with my uncles and their drinking buddies at Ashton's grocery store on the corner, just up the street from my grandmother's house. There, while we listened to country music on the radio, my uncles sat in wooden rocking chairs, drank Miller High Life beer for hours at a time, and discussed the events of the day with their cronies. The lives and habits of black people were a frequent topic of conversation. I heard over and over again that "Niggers were no account and lazy" and that they didn't take care of the children that resulted from their indiscriminate sex. I learned that most black people relied on welfare checks to get by, which they routinely squandered during drinking binges, when they shot and cut each other with razors for entertainment.

It's ironic to realize that all or most of the criticisms that were being leveled at black people by my uncles and their friends could have perhaps more legitimately been leveled at them. For the most part, they were poorly educated, blue-collar workers struggling to get by in the world. I suppose that my uncles and their friends made themselves feel better by trashing blacks, who were struggling just as hard, if not harder, to make some kind of decent life for themselves and their families.

After a time, my grandmother fell ill and was unable to care for my sister and me while my mother was at work. Because we were too young to be left alone, my mother was forced to place us temporarily in the Junior House, the county home for orphans and other children who had no one to care for them.

The time I spent at the Junior House was one of the most miserable times of my life. I remember being confused when I found out that I couldn't leave with my mother when she left that first day. I still recall what it was like to go to bed every night and wake up every day feeling unloved, unworthy, insignificant, and powerless. I will never forget what it felt like to be called to the front of a first-grade classroom to receive a free lunch ticket or to wear shirts made out of Purina chicken feed sacks.

I don't remember how long my sister and I stayed at the Junior House—my mother was never predisposed to discuss those times—but I am truly grateful for the experience. I am grateful because I feel that the experience helped me transcend the ignorance and hateful arrogance that typified my early family environment. Being a ward of the Junior House taught me what it felt like to be stripped of my dignity and sense of worth as a human being—what it felt like to be an outsider, an "other." At the very least, the Junior House experience helped me empathize with others who have suffered similar circumstances through no fault of their own, circumstances that may have set them apart as social outcasts in one way or another.

The most remarkable thing to me now is that during all the time I was growing up, I never once questioned the social order. Like everyone else, I became acclimated to the conditions. I assumed that things were the way they were supposed to be. No one I respected or admired or loved ever questioned the way things were. In fact, everyone I knew thought that things were exactly as they should be: that God was in his heaven and all was right with the world. Of course, I didn't know any black people.

At this point in my life, I admit that I don't have the vaguest notion of what it feels like to be black. I don't know, because I've never had to drink from a blacks-only water fountain, been forced to ride at the back of the bus, been turned away from a restaurant because of my skin color, or been restricted to balcony seating at the movie theater. I also admit that I don't know what it's like to be a woman, or a Jew, or anything else that I'm not now nor have ever been. In fact, I recognize that in some ways I'm sexist and racist and prejudiced. Although this may seem like a foolish thing for me to admit, I believe it's an extremely important admission for me, because I can't begin to address my shortcomings as a human being and a leader unless I first acknowledge that these shortcomings exist.

The truth is that I am what I am. I am a product of my genetic inheritance coupled with all that I have experienced in my lifetime. I believe I must acknowledge this truth and then work to overcome all the barriers that these circumstances have placed on me that prevent me from being able to relate in an honest and caring way with my fellow human beings, whether they be black or white, man or woman, Jew or Protestant.

I'm not ashamed to admit that I have innate prejudices. It is a natural tendency for human beings to identify most closely with others who are like them and to look with suspicion and distrust on those who are different. The more differences that exist, and the greater the degree of those differences, the greater the effort required to overcome them.

It is the height of arrogance for anyone in a position of leadership to think that he or she can put himself or herself in someone else's place and feel the things the other person feels. This is an important realization for me and for any leader because it helps guard against assuming how events and circumstances, or sometimes even a simple word or gesture, will affect others. The realization that we cannot know what it feels like to be white or black, a man or a woman, or a Jew or a Protestant unless we are those things should encourage us to seek to learn how and why others think and feel as they do before we say things or take actions as leaders that may have deleterious effects on the humanity of others.

My good friend and colleague, J. David Smith, thinks that prejudice is a kind of disease that we catch from others. In his wonderfully heartwarming and insightful book, *In Search of Better Angels* (in press), Dave explains what he means when he says that prejudice is an illness:

> Prejudice is a form of mental illness. I'm convinced of it. Unfortunately, it is often a form of shared mania that results in great hurt to those who are objects of its madness. Most people with other forms of mental illness are dangerous only to themselves. Prejudice is different. Its primary symptom is hatred of others, and those who are hated are at high risk of being hurt.

Will we ever get beyond our differences to the point that these differences will no longer divide us, but will instead serve to make us stronger as a society? Although I doubt that

I will live long enough to see us significantly strengthened by our differences, rather than weakened, I have faith that we will continue to grow in that direction.

When I was student teaching during the late 1960s, the "black is beautiful" movement came into vogue. One day, my supervising teacher was discussing the movement with the students in one of our eighth-grade English classes. She admitted that she was a little confused by the whole black-is-beautiful thing but wanted to be sensitive to the feelings of the black students. She asked a young man in the front row, "Willie, do you want to be called colored, or Negro, or black?" Without hesitation, he looked her straight in the eye and replied, "Can you just call me Willie, Mrs. Peterson?"

Take Time to Reflect

Can you admit that in some respects you are racist? Sexist? Or perhaps prejudiced in some other way? Do you feel that this is an important admission for a school leader? What have you done to help you better understand the thoughts and feelings of those who are not like you? What are you willing to do?

_____

_____

_____

_____

_____

_____

_____

_____

_____

_____

Can I Care Enough to Be My Own Best Friend?

C an I care enough to be my own best friend?" probably sounds like a ridiculous question to most people, but I can assure you that it's not. We frequently hear people say, "You know, he's his own worst enemy." But we never hear them say, "You know, she's her own best friend." I wish we would hear this! Of all the friends we can ever have in our lives, none is so important as the friend that we can be to ourselves. Developing a close and supportive friendship with oneself, a friendship so supportive and caring that it could even be termed a love relationship, is an important primary life task for anyone, but especially for leaders. The nature and strength of the relationships that we are able to build with ourselves are critical because we can only give away to others those things that we already possess. If we don't have an abundance of self-love and caring, then we don't have any caring and love left over that we can give away to others. A leader without the capacity to give away love and caring is seriously handicapped!

Most of us have grown up in a highly competitive culture where criticism is much more common than praise.

For example, isn't it absurd that the silver medal winner in an Olympic competition is regarded by many as a failure? Isn't it bizarre that the human being who produces the second-best performance in the entire world in a particular sports event can be tagged with the label *loser?*

Because of the competitive nature of our society and the way we have been schooled never to be satisfied with anything less than total victory, many of us have internalized a personal style that embraces a preference for criticism. As we have been encouraged by our parents, mentors, and teachers to push ourselves to the next highest level and never to be satisfied with second best, we have in turn learned to push those around us to do the same.

In American society, the cultural norm is that we must all run faster, jump higher, compile the highest grade point ratio, look prettier, make more money, and so forth than everyone else around us. Unfortunately, there can only be one Number 1 in any category, and sadly, most of us have been made to feel from an early age that we must strive to be Number 1 in every category.

With such lofty standards to measure success, is it any wonder that most of us spend a good deal of our lives feeling like failures and making others feel like failures as well? Even in those instances where we do achieve momentary success, we can't rest on our laurels and enjoy the moment, because fame is fleeting and we have to continue to scramble for that next higher rung on the ladder.

If you don't believe that people internalize a preference for criticism, then just listen to how you talk to yourself. How often do you criticize yourself both publicly and privately for your real or imagined shortcomings? When people give you compliments, how often do you deflect the kind words by denying the substance of what they are saying? How many times have you told yourself that you're stupid or dumb, that you're not okay? If you had to give a speech to a group of people and tell them what you don't like about yourself, would that be easier than it would be for you to stand up in front of that same group and tell them about your good points? Typically, it is far easier and socially more acceptable to acknowledge our weaknesses than it is to acknowledge our strengths.

If most of us were to monitor our self-talk for a while, we might be surprised at how mean and unsympathetic we are toward ourselves. It's a pretty safe bet that you would never say to your best friend some of the things that you say to yourself. For example, if you were playing doubles tennis with your best friend, you would never say to him or her the kinds of things that you would say to yourself. If your friend were to double-fault or to miss an easy put-away shot, you wouldn't yell at your friend and call him or her a "bonehead" or a "clumsy idiot" or a "stupid jerk." On the contrary, you would probably reach out and give your friend a nice friendly pat on the back to comfort him or her. You would tell your friend, "It's okay. Don't worry about it. You'll do better next time!"

But if you are the one who makes the error, then you might behave quite differently toward yourself. You might yell at yourself, throw your racquet, admonish yourself to "Get your act together," tell yourself that "You are a terrible tennis player," and verbally kick yourself over and over for your failure to make the play.

You say things to yourself and treat yourself in ways that you would never treat your best friend. If you were to treat your best friend the way you treat yourself in such situations, you wouldn't have a best friend for very long! If you continue to treat yourself in such abusive ways, then you won't be much of a friend to yourself either.

I believe that the way we talk to ourselves greatly influences our self-concepts and significantly affects our capacity to be supportive and caring toward others as well; we can only give away to others what we already have. If we constantly focus our attention on our shortcomings and our failures, we won't like ourselves very much. If we magnify our faults and tell ourselves that we are "not okay," then that is precisely what we will come to believe about ourselves. We all need to learn how to provide for ourselves the same kind of support and encouragement we so willingly and generously provide for our best friends. We must raise our awareness of the relationships that we have with ourselves and strive to improve them by treating ourselves like our most special and highly valued friends. We have to pay attention to our self-talk, and in those instances where we genuinely believe that we have made mistakes and a reprimand is in order, then we need to deliver that admonition in the same way that a loving and benevolent parent would do for a child.

As Bennis (1992) believes, "They (leaders) not only believe in the necessity of mistakes, they see them as virtually synonymous with growth and progress" (p. 96). He notes that if you haven't failed, then you haven't tried very hard and that, "Everywhere you trip is where treasure lies" (p. 149). Bennis says that, "True learning must often be preceded by unlearning, because we are taught by our parents, our teachers, and friends how to go along, to measure up to their standards, rather than allowed to be ourselves" (p. 63). He reminds us that, "By examining and understanding the past, we can move into the future unencumbered by it. We become free to express ourselves, rather than endlessly trying to prove ourselves" (p. 79).

Clearly, leaders mustn't be encumbered by the need to prove themselves to others constantly or the need to prove themselves to themselves. Although we rightfully expect that leaders will make mistakes from time to time and that they will acknowledge those mistakes when appropriate to do so, it isn't necessary for leaders to be overly critical of themselves and to beat themselves up for their failures. There is always an abundance of people out there willing to do that for them. Leadership requires the freedom to express caring for others and particularly for oneself. The following are some suggested ways that leaders can express caring for themselves and in doing so, become their own best friends.

1. Always talk to yourself and treat yourself like you would a dear friend. Be kind! Be understanding! Be gentle!

Be patient! Make sure that if you must criticize, you do so with caring and concern. Remember, if you can't count on you to be on your side when things are difficult, then whom can you count on?

2. Learn how to play—not just to win, but just to play. If victory is the object of playing, then the joy of play cannot be fully appreciated. Relax and know that you don't have to prove anything to anyone when you are at play.

3. Recognize your strengths, focus more on those strengths, and build from those strengths. Never underestimate your strengths or overestimate your weaknesses. We are all better at some things than we are at others. We need to appreciate our good points more and abandon the self-defeating drive to be the best at everything all the time.

4. Celebrate and enjoy your successes (even small successes) as well as the successes of others. When you accomplish something that you have set out to do, reward yourself by saying nice things to yourself, sending yourself flowers, taking yourself out to dinner at a nice restaurant, giving yourself a day off from work, or buying yourself a new tie or a new purse. Pat yourself on the back and remind yourself that you are indeed a special person.

5. Seek to maintain a state of balance between your need to be productive in your professional life and your need to be satisfied in your personal life. Remember that meaningful relationships are to be prized over plaques on the wall. To be most effective, leaders must lead full and balanced lives.

6. Strive to keep things in perspective. It's easy to let small problems grow out of proportion and to imagine that they are much more serious than they really are. When you feel unduly stressed by a problem, try to measure it against something that is really important in your life, such as the health of your spouse or the loss of a special relationship that you hold dear. In most cases, your problem will seem far less critical.

7. Make it a habit to laugh every day. When we laugh, we are giving ourselves the gift of joy. What nicer gift could we give to our best friend?

8. Make sure you have someone you can talk with frankly and honestly when the need arises. Leadership can be a lonely proposition at times. In many situations, leaders cannot share their innermost feelings with others in the workplace—sometimes, not even with family. I have a minister friend who has a "contract friend" for just such occasions. He and his contract friend meet every now and then for lunch to talk about the things bothering each of them. They are not professional colleagues, nor are they social friends. Their one connection in life is to meet, listen carefully to the other's concerns, and give unbiased and honest feedback.

9. Remember that the daily act of caring is extremely demanding and energy-consuming work. No one person has the capacity to love and care for himself or herself and everyone else in the organization all the time without a great deal of help. Seek to build a climate of caring in the workplace, where others develop a willingness to care and to share that caring freely.

10. Enjoy the journey and forget about the destination. Your life will be much more productive and less stressful if you can learn to do this.

Caring enough to become your own best friend should be a primary life goal for anyone who aspires to a leadership role. Through accepting, loving, and caring for yourself while acknowledging your strengths and weaknesses, you will discover that you possess a greater capacity to accept, care for, and even love others with whom you live and work. If we truly care enough to lead, then each of us in our own way must also care enough to become our own best friend.

Take Time to Reflect

Are you your own best friend? How do you know? Can you cite some specific examples of how you have incorporated into your life some of the ten suggestions on becoming your own best friend that are listed above? If not, what do you plan to do about it?

_____

_____

_____

_____

_____

_____

_____

_____

_____

_____

_____

_____

_____

_____

_____

_____

_____

_____

_____

Why Haven't Our Schools Been More Successful?

R ecent years have witnessed a mountain of reports from an assortment of blue-ribbon commissions, committees, and task forces declaring that American education is broken and suggesting various alternatives to fix it. *A Nation at Risk* (National Commission, 1983) was the first such report to gain widespread public attention. It sparked a flood of similar reports that in time spawned a storm of public outrage in protest to what was perceived as the failure of the American system of education. As a result of the influence of these reports on public opinion, towering waves of educational reform began to beat relentlessly against the landscape of American public school education. Since this unprecedented onslaught of public criticism, we as a society have tried about everything imaginable to improve our schools. At best, the results of our efforts have been disappointing. Why is that? Why haven't we been more successful in improving the performance of our schools? What can we do that we haven't done already, and how can we do it? These questions should be of great interest to all school leaders. They are certainly questions that I've thought about a lot. Allow me to share some of these thoughts with you now.

The first major wave of school improvement efforts followed closely on the heels of *A Nation at Risk* (National Commission, 1983) and crested in a mountain of state mandates and regulations designed to reform curriculum, academic requirements, professional licensure requirements, and performance standards for students, teachers, and schools. This first big wave was all about *reforming* American education; its focus was on raising standards while providing strict accountability measures to monitor progress.

But what were the results of these initial efforts to reform American education? Despite all the time, energy, and fiscal resources invested, most people would agree that we didn't get the results that we expected. Indeed, after a mountain of reform legislation had been implemented, schools had higher academic standards for students in terms of the number of courses required and their rigor. There were more and longer days in the school year, tighter attendance requirements, more tests with higher standards for success, and tougher requirements to enter and remain in the teaching profession. But when this first big reform wave receded from the educational landscape, what remained for the most part was a great deal more work, frustration, and stress for teachers and administrators and only modest gains for students.

The assumption that drove the first big reform wave was that the chief problem with American education could be found in watered-down curricula, low academic standards for students, and lax accountability for teachers, administrators, and schools. In my view, that assumption was flawed. We learned once again that simply doing more of the same thing, even if we did it a little better, would not produce the results we were hoping to achieve.

The second major wave of school reform was aimed at *restructuring* our public schools. The intent of restructuring was to do the business of education in a different way by redesigning roles and relationships to get the job done more effectively and efficiently. In the words of Ann Lieberman (1988), the call for restructuring schools "raises issues of fundamental change in the way teachers are prepared, inducted into teaching, and involved in leadership and decision making at the school level" (p. 4). Restructuring represented an important evolution in thinking about education, because the underlying assumption behind restructuring was that the chief problem with American public school education resided in the structure of schools and the roles of teachers and principals in those schools, not in the curriculum, academic standards, or accountability measures that happened to be in place.

For the last 100 years or so, schools have operated on a nineteenth-century model that casts principals in the role of management and teachers in the role of labor. Perhaps more than anything else, this has contributed to fractured school communities where there are few shared values and no clear consensus on goals or the best means to achieve those goals. Consequently, few schools have common visions of what they can achieve. This lack of shared vision has at best limited the effectiveness of schools as organizations and at worst created adversarial relationships where teachers, principals, and staff are pulling in opposite directions, more intent on maintaining the balance of power than in achieving a common dream.

There is little doubt in anyone's mind that schools need a transformation in terms of how they are organized and how people in them work together to meet the needs of students. The crucial question is, how can this transformation take place? Despite the intense efforts to restructure schools, for the most part the results have been no less disappointing than they were with the first major wave of reform. A logical conclusion could be that maybe it's not enough to change the way organizations are structured, just as it wasn't enough to raise standards and increase accountability measures.

The most recent major reform wave is still cresting, although we are beginning to feel its ominous presence as it begins to sweep across America. This reform wave, termed *reinventing education*, had its origins late in the Bush presidency

(1989–1992) with the president's proposal to create 435 "break-the-mold" schools across America. The break-the-mold schools were to be cooperative ventures primarily involving leadership in government, business, and industry. The hope was that from this cooperative effort (which excluded educators for the most part), new models for education would emerge that would totally redesign elementary and secondary education as we know it and thereby assure that America would retain its status as Number 1 in the world's pecking order economically, politically, and militarily.

For better or for worse, political fortunes shifted, and the break-the-mold schools were never funded by Congress; however, the idea of reinventing education has continued to grow in popularity over the past decade.

The idea behind reinventing education is that American schools are so bad that it's folly to try to tweak them simply by raising standards or restructuring them to make them serve our purposes better. Those who favor reinvention feel that the institution we know as public school education has outlived its usefulness and needs to be completely demolished and rebuilt from the ground up. This sentiment has taken a number of forms in recent years, including departures from the mainstream to create choice schools, charter schools, schools operated for a profit by private concerns, and even universities taking over schools and running them.

It's still a little too early to predict the results of these experiments. Choice and charter schools are increasing rapidly, but it will be a while yet before we will know the effect of these experiments on the children they serve and don't serve and the society that sanctions them. Businesses operating schools for profit have recently taken some significant blows with the cancellation of their contracts with several urban school districts. In my opinion, the future does not look particularly promising for similar efforts.

To recap briefly, we have witnessed several major movements or waves designed to improve American education in the past fifteen years. The first major attempt at school improvement, the reform movement, attempted to raise standards and improve accountability. The second major initiative, restructuring, involved redesigning roles, responsibilities, and relationships. The third major wave of school improvement, reinvention, was concerned with wiping out the old and creating a brand-new American institution to serve the educational needs of our youth. A lot of good thinking, time, energy, and resources have been devoted to these efforts to improve American schools. But the question still remains: Why haven't we been more successful?

I believe that some of the answers to this question are pretty obvious. In planning and implementing the first reform wave, all we did was more of what we had already been doing. And we all know that if you do what you did, you'll get what you got. A second reason school improvement efforts have not produced the results we had hoped for is that society may simply be asking schools to do too much. When schools don't measure up to the unrealistic standards placed on them, they are criticized unmercifully. Times have changed, and so have the clients that schools must serve. Schools are beleaguered by a flood of social problems plaguing children and young people: alcohol and drug abuse, teen pregnancy, juvenile violence, adolescent suicide, homelessness, and poverty. If one considers the range of social problems facing our youth and then places them in the context of the academic demands of an increasingly complex, modern society, then the enormity of the task begins to take form. It's no wonder that private enterprise hasn't been able to produce results superior to those achieved by our existing public schools. If it were that easy, those of us in public education would have already done it!

There are of course other reasons why schools have struggled to produce the results that society demands. There is that all-time favorite of both teachers and administrators, a lack of fiscal resources. And without question, there are problems in the political structure that severely limit what schools can achieve. There are all these problems and more. No doubt they are all partially to blame for the failure of schools to measure up to society's expectations. But in my view, the most serious problem facing schools is not a lack of resources, intrusive politics, social problems, a faulty organizational structure, or anything else that has been discussed thus far.

The most serious problem facing our public educational system in America is a lack of collective willpower that comes from a deep sense of caring about schools, children, and what schools can and should be doing for children. Until that problem is addressed, all the other solutions we have tried or will try will come up short time and time again.

To paraphrase the late Ron Edmonds, the truth is that we already know all that we need to know to educate those children whose education is of importance to us. We understand an awful lot about how human beings learn, and we have the technical expertise to apply that understanding in ways that will get acceptable results. We have the resources we need to apply our knowledge of how human beings learn if we choose to do so. America is the richest nation on earth. How can anyone even suggest that we don't have the resources we need to educate our young people?

The greatest problem we are facing in American education today is that we lack the will as teachers, as administrators, as citizens—as a society—to do what we know how to do, and can do, to educate all the children of this nation. In the final analysis, we simply don't care enough! The fundamental problem that results from a lack of caring is not a problem we can solve with our heads, it's a problem we must solve with our hearts. Until we approach the problem of caring enough to lead with our hearts, we can never be as successful in educating children as we would like to be.

In the next chapter, I describe a school where teachers, administrators, and staff do indeed lead with their hearts. I think you will agree that the results of this approach are certainly worth emulating in many other settings around the country.

Take Time to Reflect

In this chapter, I have described the reasons why I feel that American schools have been perceived as not being as successful as they need to be in educating our young people. What do you think are the main reasons for the perceived failure of American schools?

_____

_____

_____

_____

_____

_____

_____

_____

_____

_____

_____

_____

_____

_____

_____

_____

_____

_____

_____

_____

How Is a School Transformed?

At the University of South Carolina, where I worked for many years, my colleagues and I engaged in a number of research projects over twenty years in an effort to understand how schools worked so that we could help make them better places for teachers to teach and children to learn. One of the primary areas of focus for our research efforts was compensatory education.

We selected compensatory education as a focus for several reasons, including (1) a lot of resources are expended on compensatory education programs; (2) for the most part, compensatory programs have generally been regarded as largely ineffective; (3) a lot of children (especially in our part of the country) were being served by these ineffective compensatory programs; and (4) those who are served by compensatory education can be generally categorized as low-achieving, low-socioeconomic-status students who don't have many advocates to represent their interests. Unlike special education students, who come from a variety of backgrounds that straddle the social strata, compensatory students come only from poor families. In our region, that generally meant poor, black families. In this country, as in most other countries in the world, *poor* is a synonym for *powerless*. For all these reasons, we thought we should try to help.

When we first began our study of compensatory programs, we were shocked and dismayed by what we found. About fifteen years ago, my colleague, Lorin Anderson, directed a study of Chapter I schools in the region as a part of a reauthorization study for the federal government. As a part of the research design, members of his research team went into Chapter I schools and shadowed students in the program to try to understand what it was like to actually be a student in a Chapter I program. The researchers followed the children from class to class each day and noted the kinds of instructional experiences students received in a typical school day.

After a few weeks of gathering data in this way, Lorin brought his research team together in a meeting designed to let researchers share the early results of their efforts. One of the research team members began to report on the things she had been observing. The more she talked about what she had witnessed, the more emotional she became, until she was sobbing inconsolably. She was weeping for all the first- and second-grade children who were intellectually wasting away in Chapter I programs in the schools she had visited. She saw them as academically dead, doomed to a lifetime of failure in school and in life. She knew in her heart that these children were not getting the things they needed from their school experiences to allow them to live satisfying and productive lives, and it hurt her deeply.

The experience with the Chapter I reauthorization study led us to conduct a large study of remedial and compensatory programs in South Carolina for the Education Improvement Act (EIA) Select Committee, a blue-ribbon oversight committee charged with monitoring the progress of the massive Education Improvement Act enacted by the General Assembly in South Carolina in 1984. The state was expending considerable funds on compensatory and remedial education, and the select committee wanted to know what the people of South Carolina were receiving for their money.

Without going into exhaustive detail, some of the results of our study were disturbing, if not downright shocking. For example, we discovered that the standards that the state had set to judge whether individual schools were successful or unsuccessful in their compensatory programs were so low as to be meaningless. Under the state standards, to be successful, a school had to achieve one normal curve equivalency (NCE) gain on average for two of three years on standardized tests in reading and math. Under these standards, approximately 95% of the compensatory math programs in South Carolina were judged successful, and 90% of the compensatory reading programs were termed successful. When we reviewed the progress of students who had been placed in compensatory programs, however, we found that about two-thirds of them either spent their entire academic careers in compensatory programs or returned to them periodically throughout their school years. Because the purpose of compensatory education programs is to give students the knowledge and skills they need to return to and remain in the academic mainstream, the numbers didn't add up.

Based on this information, I asked the state superintendent of education a simple question: How can 95% of the programs be successful, while two-thirds of the students are failures? This was not a question to which the chief state school officer cared to respond.

We found some other problems in the compensatory programs that we felt were significant and needed to be addressed. For example, when we analyzed the curricula being taught to students in compensatory programs, we found that students were being taught approximately two grade levels below those on which they were being tested with standardized tests. Consequently, even though students successfully passed their work in school, they were doomed to failure on the standardized tests. Given these circumstances, it was little wonder that so few of them exited compensatory programs and returned to and remained in the academic mainstream.

Needless to say, the results of our study created quite a stir in the halls of government. The chief result of our painstaking work was that most of those connected with compensatory programs spent the majority of their efforts trying to save face rather than directing those efforts at improving the programs. We were depressed by all this and decided that we would change our tack. Rather than studying programs that were unsuccessful, we would go in an entirely different direction and study some programs that were successful. This provided me with the rare opportunity to see something quite wonderful: schools that had been transformed!

When we reviewed the compensatory test results in our state, we discovered that twelve schools had achieved with their students not just an NCE gain, but double-digit NCE gains in reading and/or math for three consecutive years. These were astounding results! The big question was, how did they do it? We decided to find out.

After reviewing data on the twelve schools, we selected four schools for further study and sent teams of researchers to each of the four to observe in classrooms, conduct interviews, collect artifacts, and so forth. I was a member of the team that visited an elementary school I will call Zenia Elementary. Let me describe for you some of the things we saw and felt when we visited Zenia Elementary, a living example of a school that has been transformed.

When we entered the school for the first time, there was a special feeling that seemed to be radiating from the building itself. It came from the hallways, the cafeteria, the office complex. The building seemed to be saying to us, "This is a different kind of school." Something was going on here.

There was something in the air, but we didn't know exactly what it was. We could feel it, but at the time, we couldn't begin to decipher or even to describe it. Arranged on the walls on each side of the hallway, stretching from the front entrance to the main office area, were self-portraits of the children. All the faces seemed to be happy and smiling. The school's maintenance engineer greeted the research team at the entrance and conducted us to the administrative offices. He had been briefed and knew that we were coming, and he expressed his pleasure that we would be in "his" school for several days. He gave the impression that he was not only proud to be a staff member at Zenia, but that he knew that he was also fortunate to be a part of something special. This kind of feeling was subsequently reflected in conversations with all the staff members and most of the students we met during our visit to the school.

My initial encounter with the maintenance engineer, as well as my interactions with other staff members, reminded me of Margaret Wheatley's (1992) ideas concerning the existence of invisible fields in organizations that occupy all the space that appears to be empty to the naked eye. These fields are filled with tiny particles or waves or forces, like those found in magnetic fields or radio transmissions, for example. These invisible forces are present in the vacant spaces of organizations, and they constantly signal the vision that is the essence of the organization. Wheatley believes that everyone in the organization, whether consciously or unconsciously, is constantly sending out signals that serve to form these fields:

> Now, we need to imagine ourselves as broadcasters, tall radio beacons of information, pulsing out messages everywhere. We need all of us out there, stating, clarifying, discussing, modeling, filling all of space with the messages we care about. If we do that, fields develop—and with them, their wondrous capacity to bring energy into form. . . . If we have not bothered to create a field of vision that is coherent and sincere, people will encounter other fields, the ones we have created unintentionally or casually.
>
> It is important to remember that space is never empty. If we don't fill it up with coherent messages, if we say one thing but do another, then we create dissonance in the very space of an organization. (pp. 55-56)

There was no dissonance in the fields radiating throughout Zenia Elementary. Everyone was sending the same signals about the things they cared most about. We found out exactly what those things were in our first interview, which was conducted with the man who had been principal of the school for sixteen years.

The principal, whom I shall refer to as Dave, was a bundle of energy and commitment. When we asked him to explain the extraordinary success of his school in educating compensatory youngsters, he thought about the question for a moment before he replied. Then he said, "When I became principal of this school sixteen years ago, I looked around me, and I didn't see a school for children. I said to the teachers, 'Do you want this to be a school for children? If you will help me, then we can make it so.'" He then proceeded to tell us how they had organized their compensatory program to make certain that children would be successful.

The keystone of their vision for children was a simple declaration: *No child will fail.* The administration, teachers, and staff had all bought into the notion that the school would have zero tolerance for failure and that no child would be allowed to fail, no matter what the circumstances. The rest was almost easy.

Because compensatory students were the most academically needy students in the entire school, the decision was made that they should receive the best resources the school had to offer. That meant that the compensatory students would get the very best teachers, the most enriched curriculum, the finest materials and supplies, and the most desirable classrooms. To say the least, this is atypical of most of the compensatory programs with which I am familiar. At Zenia Elementary, it became a cherished honor to be asked to teach the compensatory students, because only the very best teachers were entrusted with these children. At the end of the year, the compensatory teachers received a standing ovation from their colleagues for the wonderful work they had done with their students.

Can you even begin to imagine what it must feel like, what a marvelously confirming personal and professional experience it would be, for a teacher to receive a standing ovation from his or her colleagues? The year that we visited Zenia Elementary, 98% of the compensatory students from the previous year had tested out of the compensatory program by the end of the first grade, which was the grade level on which their program concentrated. Not only did they test out of the compensatory program, but their test scores fell at the midpoint or above in relation to all the students at their grade level who had been tested. This insulated them from the likelihood that they would fall back into the compensatory program at some later date in their school careers.

When the test scores came in and the staff learned that they had achieved a 98% success rate, Dave said to them, "Colleagues, we've done a wonderful job this past year. We achieved a success rate of 98%. But you know what? If we work just a little harder, I know that we can reach 99%!" He was simply reminding the staff that at Zenia Elementary School, no child would be allowed to fail.

At Zenia Elementary, barriers that tended to isolate people from each other had been systematically removed. Interactions among students, teachers, administrators, parents, and citizens were frequent, varied, and two-way. Student personnel teams comprised of administrators, teachers, counselors, and other specialists were regularly convened to try to come up with solutions for students experiencing difficulties at school. If you think about it, doctors don't work in isolation, neither do attorneys or engineers—why should teachers? At Zenia, everyone felt a joint responsibility to work with their colleagues to make sure all students were successful.

At Zenia, a climate of caring permeated the entire school. Teachers cared for students, and students cared for teachers. Administrators cared for students and teachers, and vice versa. Everything that was done with and for everyone in the school reflected that caring. A "Love Jar" was located in the main office to collect funds to provide children from poor families with things they needed. Staff members, children, and community members all made donations. Teachers didn't want to take their sick days even when they were ill because they felt as if their students and their colleagues needed them to be there every day. It was evident that the community cared about the school and the children who were served by the school. The school boasted more than 300 active volunteers and thirteen corporate sponsors, who provided a wealth of resources to enhance the programs at Zenia.

How did this one elementary school become such a special and caring place? It wasn't an accident, and it didn't happen overnight. It was a gradual change based on a simple idea that created a vision for the school: *No child will fail.* Over the years, many small decisions were made that enhanced that vision, until it became not just an idea, but a reality.

One of the most memorable interviews during my visit to the school was conducted with the media specialist at Zenia. She told me that when the principal, Dave, had asked her to join the staff of the school a number of years before, she had initially declined. But Dave had persisted in his pursuit of her, and finally she told him, "Dave, I don't want to come to Zenia Elementary because I don't know anything about elementary schools. I'm a high school media specialist." His reply to her declaration was telling: "I don't care about the things that you know and don't know—I care about the kind of person you are. I know you are the kind of person I want to be our media specialist." So, against her better judgment, she agreed to accept the position of media specialist at Zenia. She told me how one day, she had come into the media center and wondered how it looked to a first grader. She explained that to find out, she got down on her knees and knee-walked around the entire media center to get the view from a first grader's perspective.

I know why Dave hired this woman. She was exactly the kind of person who would share a vision that no child would fail! In the words of Peter Senge (1990):

A shared vision is not an idea. It is not even an important idea such as freedom. It is, rather, a force in people's hearts, a force of impressive power. It may be inspired by an idea, but once it goes further—if it is compelling enough to acquire the support of more than one person—then it is no longer an abstraction. It is palpable. People begin to see it as if it exists.

Few, if any, forces in human affairs are as powerful as shared vision. (p. 206)

What happens when a vision is shared by everyone in a school? When this happens, then the people in the school become connected in an essential way. The school derives power from this connectedness, and the shared vision becomes a powerful force, a force capable of transforming the school into the kind of place that we all know it can and should be. At Zenia Elementary, that was a place where children were not allowed to fail. The power that can be derived from a shared vision makes it possible for those of us in schools to deal with all the daily distractions that we routinely face, and at the same time make significant progress toward the common purpose, which is what matters most to those of us who share the vision.

Sergiovanni (1992) describes the connectedness that results from a shared vision in terms of a learning community that "resembles what is found in a family, a neighborhood, or some other closely knit group, where bonds tend to be familial or even sacred" (p. 47). In such a school, bureaucratic lines are blurred, and the need to manage people is reduced because people manage themselves in accordance with the shared vision. In the rare instances where this kind of fundamental change in structure occurs, schools are truly transformed and become "virtuous enterprises," according to Sergiovanni:

When purpose, social contract, and local school autonomy become the basis of schooling, two important things happen. The school is transformed from an organization to a covenental community, and the basis of authority changes, from an emphasis on bureaucratic and psychological authority to moral authority. To put it another way, the school changes from a secular organization to a sacred organization, from a mere instrument designed to achieve certain ends to a virtuous enterprise. (p. 102)

The virtuous enterprises that schools can become are invariably structured in such a way that caring is reflected throughout the entire school community. This is never an accident: Caring organizations are created by design. As Chaskin and Rauner (1995) suggest,

We must search for mechanisms to build caring into the environments and activities in and through which young people develop. We need to determine how we can organize our institutions and actions so as to foster and support our caring behavior. (p. 719)

If one can accept the premise that building caring organizations is never an accident, but rather the result of a collective vision, one must also come to the realization that the process of arriving at that collective vision is never easy. The principal of Zenia Elementary built that school's vision with his faculty over a period of sixteen years. I'm constantly amazed that people assume that the process of vision building is a whole lot easier than it is in reality. Many people are absolutely convinced that the leader can and should craft a vision for the organization in her or his brain and then magically transfer that vision to everyone who is a part of the organization. And then, of course, they should all live happily ever after!

When I was interviewed for my current position as Dean of the School of Education, I was asked the following question by a member of the search committee: "What is your vision for the School of Education and Organizational Leadership at the University of La Verne?" "Finally," I thought, "a question that doesn't require a great deal of thought on my part." I immediately replied, "I don't have one!" (By the way, in most instances, this is probably the wrong response if you want to be the successful candidate for a leadership position, since most people tend to believe that a leader should be—above all else—a visionary!) When pressed to justify why I didn't have the requisite vision at hand, I explained that it would be both presumptuous and foolish for me to assume that I could frame a vision for another person and beyond foolish to assume that I could pull a vision out of a hat for a whole organization full of people. However, I did assure the search committee that I felt very capable of working effectively with others over time to frame a vision for the School of Education and Organizational Leadership. Of course I had a pretty good idea of what I thought a school like ours could and perhaps should be. But at the same time, I realized that it's simply not possible to arrive at a vision for an organization without embarking on a journey of discovery with all those who will be dramatically affected by that vision.

Zenia Elementary School was a virtuous enterprise, where all the employees did, in fact, seem more like volunteers than they did employees. All of us who visited the school and witnessed the power of the shared vision were convinced that this was true. In all my years in education, I don't believe I've seen another school where all the teachers and other staff members refused to take sick days because they were convinced that their students and their colleagues needed them to be in school every single day. That kind of dedication is what we see from people who identify so much with the values of the workplace that they are more like volunteers than employees. De Pree (1989) says that the best people in organizations are more like volunteers than employees. Because they are like volunteers, these people "do not need contracts, they need covenants" (p. 28).

There could be more schools like Zenia Elementary if people cared enough to make it so. How about your school? Is it a virtuous enterprise? Have you and your colleagues come to the understanding that the most important thing in life is deciding what's most important? Are the people who work in your school more like volunteers than employees? Do you and your colleagues have a shared vision for what a school can be? Are your priorities in line with that vision? Do you accept your responsibility to act like a tall radio beacon beaming out a positive message in all directions, a message that will help to create a field of caring and concern for everyone in the total school community?

Take a Moment to Reflect

See if you can determine what the "official vision statement" is for your particular organization. Do you feel that this is an appropriate vision for your organization? If not, write the vision statement you would propose for your organization in the space below.

_____

_____

_____

_____

_____

_____

_____

_____

_____

_____

_____

_____

_____

_____

_____

_____

19

Why Am I a Professional Educator?

For five years, I lived next door to the world's greatest medical supplies salesperson. I kid you not! This guy was an absolutely incredible medical supplies salesperson. For seven out of eight years, he was recognized as the national salesperson of the year by his company. Because of his extraordinary performance, he was frequently offered promotions to management positions by his company, which he politely declined. He turned down the promotions because he loved to sell medical supplies, and it showed—not just in sales quotas exceeded, but in financial rewards accrued as well.

Because of his success, my neighbor Joe had to find places to put his money. He owned four other houses he rented out in our neighborhood, shares in other real estate ventures, and a place at the lake. One year, Joe bought a lot on the golf course at Edisto Island, South Carolina, where he built a beautiful vacation home for his family. He purchased eight or nine cars while he was my neighbor. These were mostly BMWs, with a Cadillac and a few off-road vehicles, station wagons, and trucks mixed in for good measure. He owned three boats of various sizes, which he selected for use in terms of the particular nautical activity he was planning. This guy was incredibly successful!

Despite his business success, one could not feel even the slightest tinge of jealousy toward Joe. In fact, those of us who knew him well were happy for his success because he was just the kind of person who deserved it. Not only was he a great salesperson, he was a terrific guy, a good neighbor, father, husband, and friend. Joe was a great, big, old teddy bear: six feet, five inches, with a ready smile that was wider than he was tall. He was a sensitive, kind, and generous human being with the power to draw people to him like a magnet (maybe that's why he could sell medical supplies so well).

There were many benefits associated with being Joe's neighbor. For example, he always included me on his annual week-long fishing excursion on the inland waterway near Beaufort, South Carolina, and I frequently got an opportunity for first refusal on his cast-off consumer goods when he decided to upgrade or update. I purchased three BMWs and a boat from Joe during the five-year period that I lived next door to him. All these benefits were wonderful, but maybe the best thing of all about being Joe's neighbor was that he and his wife had three incredible little boys who were perfect playmates for my two elementary-school age sons.

When it came to playing together, his boys and my boys fit together like the fingers of one hand interlaced with the fingers of another. The kids ranged in age from about four to ten, loved the same games, and seldom argued or fought with each other. My sons loved being over at Joe's house; in fact, they did just about everything but take their nightly baths and sleep there. I kept telling myself that the main reason that all the kids played at Joe's house was because his children had all the latest toys and gadgets known to humankind, in addition to a well-stocked refrigerator. Joe's kids had access to a regulation pool table, a big-screen television, a VCR, and all the characters and paraphernalia ever invented for GI Joe, Masters of the Universe, and Star Wars as each, in turn, became popular with American youngsters.

One day, my eldest son, Patrick, who was about ten or eleven at the time, came home from a great day of fun, food, and frolic over at Joe's house. He walked into the house beaming and declared, "You know, Dad, if I could pick anybody in the world to be my father, it would be Joe!" To my credit, I laughed out loud as I replied, "Me, too, Patrick! Me, too!" More than fifteen years have slipped by since my firstborn uttered these words to me, but I still occasionally remind him of them when I want to get his goat. (What I never tell him is that there were times during his mid- to late-teenage years when his mother and I would have gladly traded him for almost any other kid in the neighborhood. His reaction to Joe when he was a young child was certainly understandable, and I'd like to think that, just like my wife and me, most other parents would gladly trade their offspring if given the opportunity at certain times during their children's developmental years.)

The kind of success that Joe enjoyed can make a normal person question some of his or her life choices, especially in terms of career. Although Joe was incredibly successful, he made it look effortless. When I would leave for work in the mornings, Joe's car would be parked in his driveway. Most days, when I would return home from work, his car would be parked in his driveway. During the summer, Joe would go on what he called his "summer schedule." On his summer schedule, Joe would take off from work at noon on Thursday, pack up the kids and his wife, and go to his vacation home at Edisto for a long weekend. It seemed as if Joe could do this every week during the summer if he chose to do so.

When I was younger, I occasionally questioned my choice of career. Once, in a period of frustration while I was serving as a high school principal, I seriously thought about giving up my career as an educator and going back to law school. If not a lawyer, then maybe I could have been a successful country and western singer. Or perhaps I could have been a sports announcer, or, who knows, maybe I could have been an astronaut. Sometimes, I even think that I could have been a damn good medical supplies salesperson—maybe not as good as

Joe, but certainly good enough to enjoy some of the same financial rewards that he and his family enjoyed.

Fortunately, whenever I have felt this way, reality has always set in, and I have come to my senses. Joe once told me he loved lying in bed at night and contemplating all those hordes of people using his medical supplies. He said he was excited by the prospect of people consuming large amounts of his gauze, Band-Aids, syringes, lap sponges, and the like. He had a sincere look on his face when he told me these things, so I believe he was telling me the truth. Maybe that's part of the reason he is such a great medical supplies salesperson and I would be a rotten one. No matter how much they paid me, the thought of people consuming large quantities of my products would simply not be enough to sustain me on a daily basis.

Like most other professional educators, I want to feel that my life counts for something, that I make a difference. I want to feel that my life has touched the lives of others in some small but significant way. When I look back over what I have accomplished in my life, I don't want to have to rely on the size of my bank balance to measure my worth as a human being. Like other professional educators I know, I want to feel that if I had never lived, the world would somehow be deprived of something valuable and important. I don't mean this as a criticism in any respect, but I've often thought that if something were to happen to Joe, then someone else would step into the breach and deliver those medical supplies without losing a beat.

Professional educators are not like medical supply salespeople or astronauts or country singers. Teachers and counselors and principals and superintendents and others in our profession help to shape lives in ways so special and unique that every single one of us is irreplaceable. That's an important part of why I am an educator.

Whenever I think that perhaps I made the wrong career choice, I like to remember students like Charles, a seventh-grade nonreader whom I taught during my first year out of college. I want to remember just how badly he needed me to help him learn to read and write so that he could learn what others had to teach him, how to express himself effectively, and eventually, how to be a fully functioning member of society. If I live to be 100, I'll never forget that last day of school when big old awkward Charles came up to me, shyly held out his hand, and opened it to reveal a purple and silver fishing lure—his thank-you gift to me for the many hours of individual attention I had given him during the school year. It was his way of thanking me not just for my help in teaching him to read but also for acknowledging his dignity as a human being.

That purple and silver fishing lure was just about the best gift I ever received from anyone. I must have caught more than 100 large-mouth bass with it over the years. Although it's too old and beat up to use anymore, I still have it in the top of my fishing box as a reminder of what it means to be a professional educator.

A couple of years ago, I was having lunch with a former student who is a district school superintendent. He had just come from an expulsion hearing for a twelve-year-old who had been having severe problems at school. A background investigation had been conducted as a part of the expulsion proceedings, and the investigation had turned up some rather revealing, if not downright shocking, information about the student who was the focus of the expulsion hearings. It seemed that this particular young man had been living with his mother and her boyfriend in a mobile home on the outskirts of town. But as my friend explained it,

> The kid doesn't really live in the trailer—he lives under it like a dog. He has his bed down there under the trailer and sleeps there every night—even during the winter! He gets up in the mornings, gets himself dressed, goes down to the bus stop, and comes on to school every day. He doesn't have any clean clothes, a bath, breakfast, or anybody who even cares enough to give him a hug and send him off to school. It's no

wonder that this kid is struggling so much at school and giving the teachers and the principal fits. The world is a cold, hostile, and uncaring place for him. I think it's amazing that he even comes to school at all. And here we (the school system) are trying to throw this young man out of school. We don't need to be throwing him out of school. We need to be finding ways to help this young man!

Because my friend is a school superintendent, he has the responsibility and the power to be able to do something for this child and others like him. All professional educators have that kind of power and responsibility (on one level or another) to help children like the young man in this story. In my heart, I believe that's why most of us want to be professional educators.

As I related earlier in this book, I spent a year in the Philippines as a Fulbright Fellow in the mid-1980s. When I returned to my job in the United States, I was asked to write a piece about my experiences in Asia for the department's newsletter. I can still remember how glad I felt to be an American citizen and how aware my experiences in the Philippines had made me of the power of an education to improve the quality of a person's life. I remember that I was more proud than I had been in my entire life to be a teacher with the opportunity to touch others on a daily basis and help change their lives for the better. These feelings led me to write the following words for our newsletter:

Teaching is without a doubt the greatest of the helping professions. While it's true that a competent physician can heal a broken bone, a skilled attorney can conjure up a sound argument for a suspended sentence. A man of the cloth can give one hope, if not for this life, then at least for a life to come. All these things are wonderful and beautiful in their own right. But a good teacher! A good teacher can give a child power over his or her own life. To me this is infinitely more wonderful and more beautiful!

Take Time to Reflect

Corporations are guided by boards of directors that are composed of people who are knowledgeable in the ways of business. These boards make important decisions that influence the lives of corporations in very profound ways. In many respects, much like corporations, the life a person is influenced and shaped by a "personal board of directors."

The individuals on this personal board of directors are knowledgeable in the ways of life. At key points in our lives, they share their knowledge and wisdom and influence us in ways that have a profound impact on the direction of our lives. The illustration in Figure 19.1 represents a meeting of your personal board of directors. On each line, which represents a chair at the table, write the name of a key individual who has had a profound influence on the person you have become. Feel free to add chairs if you wish. When you finish naming your personal board of directors, turn the page and review the questions relating to this exercise.

Figure 19.1 Board Room

My Personal
Board of Directors

_____   _____

_____   _____

_____   _____

_____   _____

Now that you have selected and seated the members of your personal board of directors, respond to the following questions:

How many medical doctors are there on your board?

How many attorneys are there on your board?

How many engineers are there on your board?

How many teachers are there on your board?

I have done this exercise many times with both large and small groups of people. When I ask each of the first three questions, typically a few hands go up in the room (sometimes none). But when I ask the fourth question, "How many of you have teachers on your personal board of directors?" every hand in the room goes up! Then when I ask, "How many of you have two or more teachers on your board?" "Three or more?" "Four?" the hands continue to go up all around the room. This is because teachers, more than any other professionals, touch lives in significant and lasting ways. This is why I am a professional educator. I cherish the privilege of touching young lives in significant and lasting ways. How about you?

20
Will That Be a Senior Coffee?

A few years ago, I received my first *senior* cup of coffee. In case this hasn't yet happened to you, I can assure you that the initial senior cup of coffee is a significant milestone in anyone's life. The feeling one derives from this experience is easily equivalent to what a young person feels that first time after turning 21 on entering an establishment where alcoholic beverages are served. That first senior cup of coffee is a genuine right of passage!

My first senior cup of coffee happened something like this. I arrived early to a scheduled meeting and decided to reward myself for my punctuality by stopping for a nice, hot cup of coffee. As I approached the service counter at the restaurant, I was greeted by a friendly young woman who asked, "May I help you?"

"Yes," I replied. "Give me a cup of coffee."

"Senior?" she asked."

"I just want a regular cup of coffee," I said, not understanding what she was asking me.

"Will that be a senior coffee?" she persisted.

"What's a senior coffee?" I asked, with what must have been a puzzled look on my face.

"Thirty-five cents," the young woman answered with a laugh.

"Good, gimme a senior cup of coffee!" I said, joining her in laughter.

I don't know how I got old enough to qualify for a senior cup of coffee without even realizing it, but I did. Maybe it's a simple case of denial—I expect my wife would probably agree with that assessment. It's not that I have a problem facing up to old age, it's just that I don't fully comprehend all the signs of my advancing years. Heck! I still put "brown" in the spot reserved for hair color on my driver's license application, and I haven't had brown hair for as long as anyone around me can remember. But I'm loyal like that. I refuse to forsake the brown hair that I was born with for the gray hair that snuck up and replaced it one night while I was sleeping.

Although I am not particularly pleased about some aspects of aging, there are a·lot of good things about being older. For example, you don't have to worry about looking great in your clothes anymore, and your kids eventually grow up and have lives of their own. Most of us become more comfortable in our professional lives as we realize we don't have to climb mountains for other people—we can pick our own mountains! At some point, we older people can even begin to feel good about our house payments in comparison to those of our younger neighbors. There are all these things to feel good about, and a whole lot more. But maybe one of the best things about growing older is both the opportunity and the inclination to become more reflective in our lives. For many of us, maturity brings with it a whole new perspective on where we've been and where we're headed, and leads us to question a lot of important choices already made or waiting to be made. This chapter focuses on some of the important questions that school leaders should be asking themselves as they strive to become more reflective in assessing the results of their leadership.

Where am I on my life's journey as a human being and a school leader? What have been the results of my thoughts, deeds, and actions on others who have trusted me to serve them in a leadership role? What are the things that I have done well—the things that I can feel good about? What are the things that I have done poorly—the things that I wish I had done differently? And perhaps most important, how can I use my successes and my failures to help me become a more faithful servant to those who have trusted me enough to allow me to lead? These are all-important questions that leaders should be asking themselves.

I am convinced that one of the critical qualities that sets those who are truly leaders apart from those who would be leaders is a personal commitment to reflect continuously on the results of their thoughts, deeds, and actions both with and on behalf of others. I believe this to be true, because personal reflection is an unmistakable sign of the kind of genuine caring and commitment required on the part of all authentic leaders. The willingness of leaders to struggle with the results of decisions they have made, to question whether or not there may have been better paths than the ones chosen, and to suffer and even agonize at times alongside those adversely affected by the consequences of poor decisions—these are all part and parcel of authentic leadership. This kind of personal reflection allows leaders to grow from their mistakes and become better and more faithful servants to those who will follow their lead in the future. Reflection allows those who would be leaders to keep the faith with those whom they serve. In the final analysis, it is the ultimate price required to earn the mantle of leader.

In his very insightful book, *Leadership Without Easy Answers* (1994), Ronald Heifetz points out what so many of us instinctively know, but frequently lose sight of: "Leadership is both active and reflective. One has to alternate between participating and observing" (p. 252). Unfortunately, many of us in leadership roles often get so caught up in actively participating in the chaotic swirl of events surrounding us that we forget all about our need to be "observers." Heifetz uses the analogy of someone dancing on a dance floor, as opposed to watching others dancing from the vantage point of a balcony. Because of the activity and the focus involved in actually dancing, a dancer is unable to be an effective observer of the dance. The dancer is probably aware of the music and the person he or she is dancing with, and perhaps some of the other dancers in the immediate vicinity. But the observer on the balcony can see so much more: a view of the big picture. The observer can see the orchestra, who is dancing and who is sitting out, and the people chatting at the refreshment table. The observer may even see someone spiking the punch or a young man stealing a kiss from his best girl over in a dark corner.

The point is, of course, that the dance is so much more complex than it appears from the particular vantage point of a single dancer. If one wants to really appreciate and understand that complexity, then it becomes necessary to periodically go up on the balcony and watch the dance below. This is as true of leadership as it is of dancing. Leaders must occasionally go up on the balcony and see the big picture. Leaders must step back and reflect so that they can act in ways that are in tune with the complexity of the dance that we know as leadership. Heifetz suggests that, "The right questions can help one get far enough above the fray to see the key patterns" (p. 253). Of course, I share the view that questions are a great way for leaders to get up on the balcony. The right questions might even allow one to venture down into the basement and observe from time to time, which is perhaps just as important as observing from a vantage point above the fray!

Because I believe that reflection is so crucial to leadership, I frequently ask my students and workshop participants to do an assignment that causes them to reflect on their own thoughts, actions, and deeds in a leadership role. The assignment involves writing an honest and forthright letter to themselves in which they critique their thoughts, feelings, and actions as leaders. Some of the key questions that have provided the structure for this book are the questions I ask them to address in their letters.

Many, if not most, people find this a difficult assignment. It's difficult because they are not accustomed to reflection. They are so busy trying to deal with the daily stresses and strains of leadership, in some cases just trying to survive, that they have never spent the time and energy to analyze the positive and negative consequences of their actions as leaders or to evaluate whether or not they are on paths that will allow them to become the kind of human beings and leaders they would like to become.

As a conclusion to these very personal letters, I ask my students and workshop participants to make a commitment to themselves: a commitment to do some tangible things to improve themselves as human beings and as leaders. I ask them to spell out in detail those things they are committed to doing in the days and weeks and months ahead and to attach time lines so that something will actually happen and they will move themselves in the directions they wish to go.

When my students and workshop participants have finished their letters, I have them address the letters to themselves, seal them in envelopes, and give them to a friend. They are told to instruct their friends to mail the letters to them at some time in the future when the friends feels that they need a little boost to get back on track and strive harder to realize the promises they have made to themselves.

I have done this exercise on a number of occasions myself. Invariably, I am surprised at the things revealed to me. Occasionally, when I ask myself the question, "What do I care about?" I find that the answer is not the answer I want it to be for me. Maybe I find myself caring about things that are small and inconsequential in the big scheme of things. Although I hate to admit it, I may find myself caring about personal recognition or personal comfort. Or perhaps when I ask myself the question, "Why am I doing this?" I don't like the answer because I learn that my actions are motivated by a desire to exercise power over others or to show off my superior knowledge or skill in a particular area.

Although I may not like the answers I receive when I ask these kinds of questions, it is critical that I ask them if I expect to become more like the person and the leader that I ultimately want to be. I have always believed that if a person genuinely cares about others, then that person will tell them the things that they need to hear rather than the things they want to hear.

Without honest and accurate feedback to guide our future actions, how can we expect to become better at the things we do and ultimately to become more like the person we want to be? If we can care enough about others to tell them the things they need to hear, can we honestly be satisfied with doing any less for ourselves? I don't think so—do you?

I am at a point on my personal life journey where I am continually struggling to make major decisions in my professional life and my personal life. Three years ago, I made a decision to leave the University of South Carolina, where I had been a member of the faculty for more than twenty years, and move to another setting where the goals of the organization were more in tune with my own. Clearly, the goals of the University of South Carolina were not the same goals that attracted me to the institution more than twenty years before, and I needed a change if I wanted to be the best person I could be. How long will I be in my present environment? I don't know. Maybe there will come a perfect time for me to move on—to become a country singer like I've always wanted to be (for all the people who've heard me sing, relax, I'm only kidding), or to pen the great American novel that we all secretly wish we could write. Maybe one day soon I will spend all of my time working as a volunteer so I can be certain that I am doing the things that I am doing because I am convinced that they need to be done, rather than because I get paid to do them. Whatever the decisions about my professional life might be, I know that we all have only a limited amount of time to make those decisions. Otherwise, external circumstances will decide these things for us.

Many important changes are also taking place in my personal life. What will be the effect of these changes in the years ahead? At long last, my children are grown men. For better or for worse, I have done the parenting thing about as long and as well as I can do it. My relationship with my children will continue to evolve in a different direction—it will never again be what it was in the past. How will I relate to my children in the years ahead? Can I find the strength and understanding to let them be the people they choose to be rather than the people I would have them be? If I am ever to have peace in my soul, I have no choice but to realize that I have no control over their lives; control over the lives of others is always an illusion. What about my relationship with the beautiful, caring, and talented woman I have been married to for the past thirty-five years? What will be the direction of our relationship? Will each one of us have the will and the resources required to continue to reshape and revitalize the relationship in such a way that it will not only endure, but will be more satisfying and rewarding than it has ever been before? I admit I don't know the answer to any of these questions. But I'm pretty sure that these are some of the questions that I ought to be asking myself about my personal life and professional life at this precise moment in time.

At the same time all these critical questions are swirling in my brain, I find myself realizing that the answers that have worked for me in the past may not be the answers that will work for me in the future. Although I may not have definitive answers for my questions, there is one thing that I do know for sure: I haven't yet done enough in my life in a number of areas. I have not done enough as a friend, a colleague, a teacher, or a leader. I have not yet done enough as a father or a husband or a citizen of the world. I'm not unduly troubled by this realization, because it helps to reassure me that I will have plenty of important work to do in the years that remain. I believe that I have the potential to be a better person than I am today. I believe that we all do.

But positive change is never easy. If any of us hopes to change anything for the better (and that's what leadership is all about), then several things must take place.

First, we must become aware of the nature of the problems that we are facing. We can't hope to solve problems if we aren't even aware that they exist. If we want things to be better than they are, then we have to make ourselves aware of the essential problems in our organizations and in our lives. As the contents of this book suggest, we must constantly question the status quo to accomplish this purpose.

The second thing that must occur to make positive change happen is that we must genuinely want things to be different. Many people are perfectly satisfied with the status quo. They are comfortable and secure and happy with the way things are at present. Positive change cannot occur in an environment where people are satisfied with the status quo.

The third and perhaps the most essential ingredient necessary for positive change to occur is a willingness to make personal sacrifices to move forward. People have to be willing to give up something—to sacrifice some of their comfort, their time, their energy, and perhaps even some of their legitimate power—for positive change to occur.

Finally, there must be a realization that change is difficult. Successful change requires commitment, persistence, and a certain measure of faith. Important changes don't happen easily, and they don't occur overnight.

As people dedicated to making a difference in the lives of others, leaders must believe that where they've come from as a person or as an organization or where they are at present isn't nearly as important as where they're headed.

When I was a principal, our school district held a celebration to recognize 200 years of public education. We did a series of skits to demonstrate how far we had come during that period in providing educational services to children. We had a theme song that tied the skits together as we moved from one era to the next in recounting the history of public schooling in the district. The chorus for our theme song was, "It ain't where you start—it's where you finish!"

I believe that. Just like human life, organizational life is a journey. Leaders need always to be asking, "What is possible for me and for all the others in this organization?" Leaders need to be eternally searching for the answers to questions such as, "What do I stand for?" What do we stand for?" "What can I be?" "What must I be?" "What can we be? "What must we be?"

Over the past thirty-five years, I have been fortunate to have had many opportunities to travel around the country and occasionally around the world to interact with others serving in various kinds of formal and informal leadership roles. Although I believe that leaders everywhere are struggling with the same kinds of problems, the ways in which they approach these problems are as varied as the surroundings in which these leaders find themselves. At this point in my life, I am convinced that there are no pat answers that anyone can offer leaders to help make their tasks more manageable or that will help lighten the burdens of leadership that weigh heavily on their shoulders.

Although I am forced to acknowledge that there are no pat answers, I am at the same time heartened by my belief that there are vast constellations of important questions that leaders can rely on to help them find their way in even the most uncertain of times and circumstances. Just as a bright star radiating its brilliance across thousands of light years of time and space can provide guidance to a sailor lost in a vast sea, key questions such as, "What do I care about?" and "What do I believe about people?" and "Why am I doing this?" can help point the way for leaders struggling to fulfill the sacred promises they have made to those who have trusted them enough to allow them to lead. It is indeed far better to know some of the questions than all the answers! Although answers come and go like the changing of the seasons, the most critical questions remain eternal and serve as faithful beacons for leaders with the commitment and the courage to ask them.

Take Time to Reflect

If we as leaders and human beings have some measure of immortality in this life, it is manifested in the impact that we have on the lives of others. Our immortality is measured in the lives we are privileged to touch and to change in positive ways as we carry out our duties and responsibilities as professionals, friends, family members, and so forth. Suppose for a moment that for some reason, you are no longer a part of the organization where you are currently employed. Or suppose that you are no longer there as a spouse or a parent or in some other role that is important in your life. Imagine that in five years you could come back and listen, unseen, while others talk about you in terms of what you meant to the organization or the family or to whatever entity you are imagining. What would you want to hear people say about you? What are you doing to build this legacy? What are you willing to do?

_____

_____

_____

_____

_____

_____

_____

_____

_____

_____

_____

_____

_____

_____

_____

_____

Your Leadership
Becomes You!

I was fifteen years old when I finally realized that I was never going to play center field for the Brooklyn Dodgers. This realization came to me rather suddenly and was the result of making three errors in the field during the first two innings of my inaugural high school varsity baseball game. The unfortunate truth was that I didn't have what it took to become a big-league baseball player. Wanting to be a professional baseball player just wasn't enough; becoming a big-league ballplayer took a lot more talent than I possessed. Like it or not, I was going to have to set my sights on being something else besides a sports hero.

Coming to the conclusion that I was never going to replace my hero, Duke Snider, as the center fielder for the Dodgers was painful. Like a lot of other young boys growing up in the 1950s and 60s, sports were the most important thing in the world to me. Athletics were a big part of my life, and ballplayers were my chosen role models. Because I strongly identified with professional athletes, I wanted to be just like them in every way possible. I tried to walk like they walked, dress like

179

they dressed, and talk like they talked. I would have loved to have gone around town with a big chaw of chewing tobacco tucked smugly in my cheek, but I was certain that my mother would have killed me if I'd tried it.

Walking and dressing and talking and even chewing tobacco like big leaguers wasn't enough to make me a professional baseball player. Being a professional baseball player also required a high degree of speed, agility, strength, and coordination. These things I wasn't able to mimic, and therefore I couldn't realize this particular dream. Fortunately or unfortunately, my desire to chew tobacco and imitate the lives of big-league ballplayers ceased with the three errors. From that day forward, my life went in a different direction.

My attempts to mimic the lives of those who were my role models were not unique to me. All my friends did it in one way or another. Although a lot of them wanted to become professional athletes, some wanted to become the next Elvis, while still others wanted to become doctors, lawyers, or Indian chiefs. The point is that we all wanted to be something when we grew up, and we lived our lives for the most part in the ways we thought we needed to live them to reach our goals, no matter how ridiculous or unreachable those goals might have been. By the way, I recently attended my thirty-fifth high school reunion, and although our class didn't produce any professional athletes, a number of my classmates had achieved a good many of their childhood dreams in one way or another.

How do we achieve our dreams? How do we learn to do something that we want to do or to be something that we want to be in life? How do human beings gain the knowledge and skills and attitudes necessary to function in the various roles they are required to fill to live full and productive lives? How does one become a successful friend, mother, teacher, lover, leader, or any one of the dozens of other starring and supporting roles that human beings are expected to play at various points in their lives?

Primarily, we all learn to function in various roles by emulating others whom we regard as being successful in those roles. We learn by doing what we have seen others do in particular situations and making adjustments in our future behaviors based on trial and error. When we experience a new role for the first few times, we have to be content with role-playing what we think a competent person would do in that particular role in that particular situation. This role play is based on a number of factors, including how we have seen others act in similar situations or what others whom we respect (parents, friends, mentors, teachers) have told us is the proper or accepted way to act. It makes little difference what the role is; it can be anything from teaching to parenting to making love. What's intriguing is that we can never be competent in any role as long as we are role-playing. It's only after we experience a metamorphosis and truly become that which we have been role-playing (teacher, parent, lover, leader) that we can reach our potential in a particular role.

Take learning to dance, for example. When we are first learning to dance, we are certainly not dancers—in fact, most of us are more like unidentified flying objects than dancers! Even learning something as simple as the box step is a considerable challenge for some of us. We watch the instructor demonstrate how to complete the box step by performing four simple movements with the feet.

While we are watching the instructor, it looks so smooth and easy. Then when it's our turn to imitate the instructor's movements, it's not as simple as it first appeared. Most of us are ill at ease and self-conscious in this situation. We watch our feet, willing them to go in the right direction. All the while, we are counting to four over and over in our heads and trying to coordinate our awkward and clumsy steps with the beat of the music.

After a time, we are ready to partner up with the instructor and move in tandem to the music. We discover that this moving together with a dance partner to the music while doing the box step is a good deal more difficult than moving to the music while doing the box step by oneself. Typically, most of us, while we are still beginners, get out of sync with the music, and sometimes we even step on the toes of our partners.

Fortunately, with enough time and practice, we can stop counting one, two, three, and four over and over in our heads as we come to realize that this pattern never varies. With some additional practice, we are usually able to stop staring at our feet as we become convinced that our feet can complete a simple box without our constant visual scrutiny, and we are comfortable in the knowledge that they aren't going to run off and hide somewhere. This is a real breakthrough on the path to becoming a dancer, because once we are able to stop counting to four while intensely supervising our feet, we are able to look at our partners, carry on a simple conversation, smile occasionally, and even listen to and enjoy the music. With enough time and practice, we can begin to innovate—to move out of the box, to turn in a circle, even to twirl our partners around. You can't *be* a dancer as long as you are watching your feet and counting your steps—you can only *do* dancing. With enough time and practice, however, most of us are able to stop thinking about what we are doing, relax, and finally enjoy the whole experience. It is precisely at this point that we stop doing dancing and become dancers.

Leadership is a lot like dancing in this important respect. As long as we are role-playing being a leader, asking ourselves questions such as, "What do the textbooks say?" or "What would some other leader do in this particular situation or set of circumstances?" we can never be leaders. We don't become leaders until we can trust ourselves enough to listen to our inner voices and know for certain that those voices will guide us in making the decisions that we instinctively know are right for us as leaders. Bennis (1992) says that becoming a leader is synonymous with becoming yourself. In his view, "Leadership is first being, then doing. Everything the leader does reflects what he or she is" (p. 141). In other words, one can't do leadership, one must be a leader. And becoming a leader is a process of evolution that is a by-product of a person living his or her life in a particular way. As Bennis notes,

No leader sets out to be a leader. People set out to live their lives, expressing themselves fully. When that expression is of value they become leaders. The point is to become yourself, to use yourself completely—all your skills, gifts, and energies—in order to make your vision manifest. You must withhold nothing. Become the person you started out to be, and enjoy the process of becoming. (pp. 111-112)

Evans (1993), while writing about the ideas of a new group of leadership theorists who emphasize the importance of authenticity in leadership, points out that, "All stress that leaders must aim not at manipulating *subordinates* who do as they're bidden, but at motivating *followers,* who invest themselves actively" (p. 21). To accomplish this purpose, Evans asserts that leaders must be more than just skillful; they must be credible. To be credible, they must first be authentic, which Evans defines as follows:

Authentic leaders link what they think, what they seek, and what they do.

They join in Sergiovanni's terms, "the head, heart, and hand" of leadership. They make their assumptions explicit about such questions as:

What basic values guide my work?
What motivates teacher performance?
How do I define my role as leader?
What are my goals for this school?
How do my actions demonstrate my values and my goals? (p. 21)

School leaders who can achieve credibility with followers through their authenticity inspire trust. They are, in the words of Evans, "leaders worth following into the uncertainties of change" (p. 21).

I agree with Evans (1993) and Sergiovanni (1992) and others who insist that leadership is much more concerned with being than it is with doing. When I first became a school principal, I mistakenly believed that I had to know how to do a lot of things well to be successful. I felt that I needed a generous supply of expert power to meet the expectations of the students, teachers, staff members, and parents who made up my school community. I was sure that I would be expected by my constituents to possess the knowledge and skills required to build perfect master schedules, design appropriate curricula, select the best staff, organize comprehensive activities programs, make wise decisions in all matters great and small, and so forth. I now know that I couldn't have been more mistaken.

Although these kinds of skills and abilities are clearly valuable assets for school leaders, they aren't the crucial factors that determine success or failure in a leadership role. Who an individual is as a human being and a leader is far more important than how much he or she knows or the set of skills he or she might possess.

People choose to follow a leader because they can identify with the leader's values. Leaders earn the trust and respect of their followers to the extent that they are able to demonstrate their allegiance to a set of universally accepted values as they carry out their daily responsibilities in a leadership role. The leader's actions serve as the confirmation that the head, the heart, and the hand are truly joined and the leader is indeed authentic, or as I like to call it, *congruent*. The knowledge and skills required to develop a perfect master schedule, design great curricula, select the best people, and so forth are not adequate substitutes for congruency, which manifests itself in things such as honesty, integrity, caring, and commitment to a set of worthwhile values. My personal life goal as a leader and a human being is to become congruent.

Let me explain what I mean by congruent by borrowing a concept from mathematics. Congruent triangles are identical. Each of the three sides as well as the three angles in congruent triangles are all equal. If one were to place one congruent triangle on top of another, the first would cover the second completely, and no overlapping areas would remain.

It is clear to me that if I am to be successful in becoming congruent in my life, then I must strive to make the person

I am on the outside identical to the person that I am on the inside, and vice versa. If I am truly congruent, then all the things that I believe or say or do will be consistent internally and externally. The people whom I come into contact with will never have to guess what I really mean or what I really think. My words and actions will be entirely consistent with my feelings and my beliefs. I will no longer be required to pretend, and I will never have to be concerned about using or manipulating others, because there will be no need to practice gamesmanship. And perhaps most important, I can become the person and the leader that I really want to be rather than constantly struggling to become the person and leader that others expect me to become. C. Michael Thompson, in his book, *The Congruent Life* (2000), emphasizes the importance of searching for the person that is you, so that you can become congruent, even if others perceive your search to be unreasonable:

> George Bernard Shaw once said that while the reasonable man adapts to the world, the unreasonable one persists in trying to make the world adapt to him. Thus he concluded, all progress depends on the unreasonable man. By that standard, we should all be unreasonable men and women. . . . If we have deep values, if we have vibrant beliefs dying to find life in what we do for a living, if we yearn for the Congruent Life— then we should insist that the world conform itself to us. (p. 269)

I have no illusions about the difficulty of the task I have set for myself. The world doesn't easily adapt to the individual, and I have already stumbled many times on my personal journey to congruency. However, I am convinced that the reward is worth the struggle. I don't care how many sides or angles ultimately define the shape of my life as long as the internal and external manifestations of who I am are congruent.

Although I may never reach my ultimate destination, I plan to take as many steps along the path as I possibly can with every passing day. Each day, I want the people in my life to feel that they can trust my leadership a little more than they could the day before, as they witness the consistency of who I say I am as a leader with the deeds that I perform in the name of leadership.

How about you? Can you force yourself to break out of that tight little box that limits your ability to lead? Can you trust yourself enough to find your own leadership style, to experiment with your own patterns and your own rhythms? Are you secure enough to be an innovator and a risk taker as you wrestle with the problems of leadership? Can you feel confident enough to stop counting your steps and to resist staring at your feet? Will you allow yourself the freedom to turn and twist and twirl as the spirit moves you? Do you accept the responsibility to serve as your own choreographer in this particular dance? Can you relax and begin to enjoy the challenges of providing leadership for those who have trusted you to lead? If someone should ask you, can you tell them why you are going to visit Bob? Finally, can you frame answers that satisfy you for most, if not all, the critical questions that have been suggested for leaders in this book?

If you can come to the realization that you can do all these things, then at that precise moment, you will be dancing the dance of a leader. You will stop doing leadership, and you will become a leader! Don't worry about stepping on a few toes here and there as you dance your dance as a leader. Remember, you're the choreographer. Only you, and you alone, can dance this unique and wonderful dance. On reflection, you will find that any missteps you make simply serve as signposts to point you in the right direction. Good luck, and remember to relax and enjoy the music!

References

Autry, J. (1991). *Love and profit: The art of caring leadership.* New York: Morrow.

Badaracco, J. L. Jr. (1997). *Defining moments: When managers must choose between right and right.* Boston: Harvard Business School Press.

Beck, L. (1994). *Reclaiming educational administration as a caring profession.* New York: Teachers College Press.

Bennis, W. G. (1992). *On becoming a leader.* New York: Addison-Wesley.

Blanchard, K., & O'Connor, M. (1997). *Managing by values.* San Francisco: Berrett-Koehler.

Block, P. (1993). *Stewardship: Choosing service over self-interest.* San Francisco: Berrett-Koehler.

Bolman, L., & Deal, T. (1995). *Leading with soul: An uncommon journey of spirit.* San Francisco: Jossey-Bass.

Bracey, H., Rosenblum, J., Sanford, A., & Trueblood, R. (1990). *Managing from the heart.* New York: Dell.

Brooks, J. L. (Producer), & Scott, T. (Director). (1996). *Jerry Maguire* [Film]. Culver City, CA: Tristar.

Burns, J. M. (1978). *Leadership.* New York: Harper & Row.

Chaskin, R. J., & Rauner, D. M. (1995). Toward a field of caring: An epilogue. *Phi Delta Kappan, 76,* 718-719.

De Pree, M. (1989). *Leadership is an art.* New York: Bantam Doubleday.

De Pree, M. (1997). *Leading without power: Finding hope in serving community.* Holland, MI: Shepherd Foundation.

Evans, R. (1993). The human face of reform. *Educational Leadership, 51,* 19-23.

Greenleaf, R. K. (1996). *On becoming a servant leader.* San Francisco: Jossey-Bass.

Handy, C. (1989). *The age of unreason.* Boston: Harvard Business School Press.

Heifetz, R. A. (1994). *Leadership without easy answers.* Cambridge, MA: Belnap Press of Harvard University.

Hogan, R., & Curphy, G. J., & Hogan, J. (1994). What we know about leadership: Effectiveness and personality. *American Psychologist, 49,* 493-504.

Lieberman, A. (1988). Expanding the leadership team. *Educational Leadership, 45*(5), 4-8.

National Commission on Excellence in Education. (1983). *A nation at risk: The imperative for educational reform: A report to the nation and the secretary of education.* Washington, DC: Government Printing Office.

Palmer, P. J. (1998). *The courage to teach: Exploring the inner landscape of a teacher's life.* San Francisco: Jossey-Bass.

Reichheld, F. F. (1996). *The loyalty effect: The hidden force behind growth, profits, and lasting value.* Boston: Harvard Business School Press.

Senge, P. (1990). *The fifth discipline: The art of the learning organization.* New York: Doubleday.

Sergiovanni, T. J. (1992). *Moral leadership: Getting to the heart of school improvement.* San Francisco: Jossey-Bass.

Simpson, D., & Bruckheimer, J. (Producers), & Scott, T. (Director). (1993). *Top gun* [Film]. Hollywood, CA: Paramount.

Smith, J. D. (in press). *In search of better angels: Stories of disability in the human family.* Thousand Oaks, CA: Corwin.

Thompson, C. M. (2000). *The congruent life: Following the inward path to fulfilling work and inspired leadership.* San Francisco: Jossey-Bass.

Vaill, P. (1989). *Managing as a performing art: New ideas for a world of chaotic change.* San Francisco: Jossey-Bass.

Wheatley, M. J. (1992). *Leadership and the new science: Learning about organization from an orderly universe.* San Francisco: Berrett-Koehler.

Index

"A Nation at Risk," 137–138
Altruism:
    leaders and, viii
    transformational leadership
        theory and, xv
Anderson, Lorin, 146
Authenticity, 16–17
Authority bases, xvi

Basic education data survey
    (BEDS) reports, 70–73
Behavioral theorists, xiv
Beliefs. *See also* Values
    faith in potential of people,
        39–40
Board of Education, Brown v.,
    122–123
"break-the-mold" schools,
    139–140
Brown v. Board of Education,
    122–123
Burns, James MacGregor, 22–23

Care/concern:
    authentic leadership and,
        169–172
    efforts of teachers and, 118–120
    importance of, 21–22, 142
    as motivational forces, 28–34
    self-love and, 129–134

significance of "little things,"
    59–65
successful compensatory
    programs and, 149–155
Change as positive force,
    173–174
Communication in home visits,
    61–62
Communities:
    home visits and, 61–62
    successful compensatory
        programs and, 151–152
Compensatory education,
    145–153
Competition, 129–134
Confidence and risk-takers, 82
Congruency, 184–185
Congruent Life, The, 185
Criticism, 129–134

De Pree, Max, 17, 105
Decisions, 91–98
Demographics and compensatory
    education, 145–146
Discrimination, 122–127

Economics, 141–142
    of compensatory education,
        145–147
Edmonds, Ron, 142

Education Improvement Act (EIA),
    146–147
Ethics, 33–34. *See also* Values

Forman, Michael, 18
Friendship, 134

Great man theory, xiv

Heifetz, Ronald, 169
Home visits, 61–62

In Search of Better Angels
    (Smith, J. D.), 126

Leadership, 22–23
Leadership and the New Science, 4
Leadership Without Easy
    Answers, 169
Leading With Soul: An Uncommon
    Journey of Spirit, xv
Leading Without Power: Finding
    Hope in Serving Community,
    xv–xvi
Loyalty Effect, The, xv

Managing by Values, xv
Managing From the Heart, xv
McGuires, Cynthia Cervantes,
    19–21
Moral Leadership: Getting to the
    Heart of School
    Improvement, xv
Morals and leadership, 20–21,
    xvi–xvii
Motivational forces:
    care/concern as, 28–34
    need for, 41–42
Motives for decisions, 91–98

National Teacher of the Year, 18

Organizations:
    interdependence in, 85–89
    leadership responsibilities of,
    45–46

Parents and home visits, 61–62
Personal vision:
    achievement of dreams and,
        180–183
    caring for self and, 129–134
    leadership and, 16
    relationships and, 172–173
Politics and "reinventing" schools,
    139–140
Potential of people, 39–40
Power:
    formal leadership and, 54
    motives for decisions and,
        91–98
    responsibilities of positions of,
        101–105
Prejudice. *See* Discrimination

Principals:
    motives for decisions by, 91–98
    responsibilities of, 67–73
    scheduling by, 108–111
Prison inmates, 38–39
Professional development:
    importance of, 63–64
    leadership institutes, 75–79

Questioning, 3–5

Reformation. *See* Restructuring of
    schools
Responsibility, 67–73
Restructuring of schools, 138–141
Risk, 75–83

Scheduling, 108–111
Significance of "little things." *See*
    Care/concern
Situational leadership theory, xv
Smith, J. David, 126
Standards:
    Education Improvement Act
        (EIA) and, 147
    performance, 138
Stewardship: Choosing Service
    Over Self-Interest, xv

Taylor, Frederick, xiv
Teaching:
    as business of schools, 117–118
    power of, 162–163
Team-building, 75–79
Theories of leadership:
    great man theory, xiv
    situational leadership theory, xv
    traits theory, xiv
    transformational leadership
        theory, xv
Thompson, C. Michael, 185
Tobin, Walt, 17–18
Traits theory, xiv
Transformational leadership
        theory, xv

Truthfulness, 107–113

Values:
    impact of education on,
        xviii–xix
    for management, xvi
    motivational forces and,
        28–31, 184
    schools as virtuous enterprises,
        153–154
    truthfulness, 107–113
Vision:
    importance of, 24
    leadership and, 16

Wheatley, Margaret J., 4

**CORWIN
PRESS**

The Corwin Press logo—a raven striding across an open book—represents the happy union of courage and learning. We are a professional-level publisher of books and journals for K-12 educators, and we are committed to creating and providing resources that embody these qualities. Corwin's motto is "Success for All Learners."